Elizabeth Butel is a writer, art historian and freelance journalist who was a regular contributor to the *National Times*. She compiled and edited Margaret Preston's *Selected Writings*, Lloyd Rees' *Peaks and Valleys: An Autobiography*, Lewis Morley's memoir *Black and White Lies*, *The Eye of the Beholder* by Betty Roland and *50 Years of Silence* by Jan Ruff-O'Herne. Other books include *The World According to Hawke*, *Kings Cross Album*, *A Life Album*, *Hurstville Oval* and *Parkes 1983-2008*. She has also contributed to the political satires, *Balmain Boys Don't Cry* and *Balmain Boys Strike Back*. Her children's books include *It's Me, Here's Me* and *More About Me* and her radio play *The Food Diaries* was broadcast by the ABC.

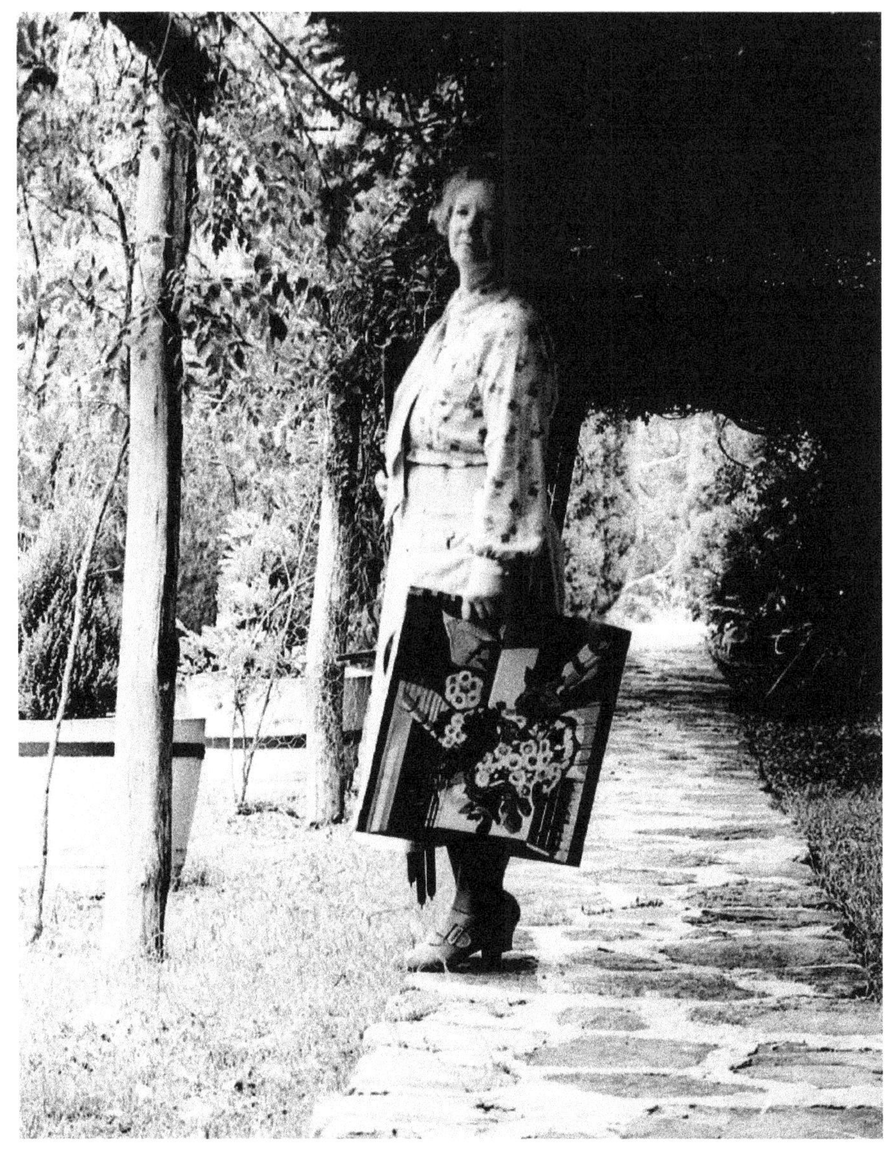

Margaret Preston at her home in Berowra, north of Sydney, 1939, as photographed by Harold Cazneaux (detail).

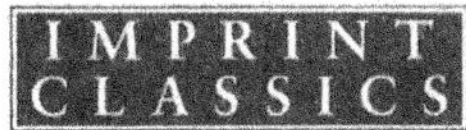

MARGARET PRESTON SELECTED WRITINGS

1920-1950

Introduced by Elizabeth Butel

ETT IMPRINT

Exile Bay

Revised 5th edition published as an Imprint Classic in 2024

First published as *Art and Australia* by Margaret Preston by Richmond Ventures in association with ETT Imprint in 2003

Published as *Selected Writings : Margaret Preston* by ETT Imprint in 2015

Reprinted 2020, 2022

First electronic edition ETT Imprint 2015

The publisher is grateful to the Trustee of the Estate of Margaret Preston and the Permanent Trustee Company Limited for granting permission to reproduce the writings and images of Margaret Preston in this book.

The editor would also like to thank Katrina Cashman and Rhonda Davis for their help in locating materials.

ISBN 978-1-923024-67-0 (pbk)
ISBN 978-1-923024-68-7 (ebk)

Cover: Margaret Preston: *Flannel Flowers*, c1929, Woodblock print.
Designed by Tom Thompson

CONTENTS

INTRODUCTION

'Wherever and whenever in the future Australian painting is discussed and evaluated, Margaret Preston will surely be one of those to be first mentioned.'[1]
HAL MISSINGHAM, August 1963

Margaret Preston died in May 1963, aged 88, leaving a large body of artwork, comprising paintings, prints and ceramics. Unlike many artists, she also left a substantial body of writing, covering the mature years of her art and life. The vigour of her opinions, well known to her contemporaries, has continued to create comment in the decades since they were written, as students and scholars of new generations discover the unique place of Margaret Preston in the history of Australian art. Excerpts from her writings have found their way into many and varied studies but it is the purpose of this collection to present a selection of her key texts in their entirety. In this way, the reader can experience her direct voice, with all its vision, paradox, and contradiction and perhaps gain fresh perspectives on how her ideas may have influenced her own art practice.

As Hal Missingham predicted, Margaret Preston is an artist for all seasons, with contemporary curators and art historians still in the process of re-evaluating her art and ideas against the shifting foci of cultural practices. Prominent among these shifting perspectives is her role in advocating for inspiration from Aboriginal and Torres Strait Islander art as a keystone for a national art, and her foresight in promoting Australia's cultural links with Asia. Assessment of her relationship to the former has been contested and recontested for the last forty or more years. It was viewed as a form of cultural imperialism in the 1980s, with Preston advising readers to appropriate designs on Tapoglyphs, shields and dance boards to decorate everyday household items and apparel, with scant regard for their cultural and spiritual significance. In the intervening decades the emergence of Aboriginal art from the margins has been accompanied by shifts in scholarly interpretation of Preston's views. One example is Andrew Sayers' comparison of her 1946 monotype, 'Bush Track NSW', to the spiritual force of a yam Dreaming painting by acclaimed artist, Emily Kngwarreye.[2]

More recently, Donna Leslie in her text on '*Margaret Preston and Assimilation*', succintly argued that Preston's perspectives and the language in which she expressed them reflected government policies of assimilation at that time.[3] With increasing scrutiny of the ethics surrounding the production and sale of Aboriginal and Torres Strait Islander art, it seems likely that Preston's ideas will continue to be interrogated in line with new understandings of her own art and that of Aboriginal and Torres Strait Islander peoples.

This collection of Preston's writings spans almost three decades, the earliest contribution in 1923, the last in 1949. These are not presented chronologically but grouped according to theme. The first section, *A Convert to Modem Art*, presents her biographical writings. The second section, *The Indigenous Art of Australia*, presents her theories about Aboriginal and Torres Strait Islander art and the role it might play in the creation of a national art. The last section, *Artists' Groundwork,* is a miscellany, comprised of selected travel writings and essays on craft and colour theories. It ends with a biographical text written at the beginning of the Second World War, where Preston recalls her experiences with 'shell-shocked soldiers' in World War 1.

Preston's writings of the 1920s are the outcome of her experiences as a mature woman; a synthesis of principles and ideas acquired both in Australia and overseas. Her writings of the 1930s could be loosely characterised as protest writings, aligned with the general tenor of small magazines of that era and the debates about nationalism that preceded World War 2. Her writings of the 1940s are more ruminative, with a new depth of appreciation added to her support for Aboriginal and Torres Strait Islander art.

The animating spirit of all the texts conforms to our impression of that 'red-headed little firebrand of a woman,'[4] described by Margaret Preston's friends and contemporaries. The voice, at its best, is fresh, direct and uncompromising; at its worst simplistic, often arrogant, and sweeping in its generalisations, employing now outmoded terms, offensive by contemporary standards. Language is often bluntly colloquial (as in the references to 'lubras' 'blacks' and 'dopey whites'.) With some notable exceptions, such as *From Eggs to Electrolux,* the writings seem direct and mostly unpremeditated, the views of a mature woman who was not shy of voicing her opinions about what she perceived as the impoverished state of Australian art and society.

The writings were published in a variety of journals, including *Art in Australia, The Home, Undergrowth, Manuscripts, Jindyworobak Review, Australia National Journal,* and various Sydney Ure Smith publications. Preston adopted a variety of styles in these, in line with the tone of the publication and its intended audience. These ranged from artless fables, as in *From Eggs to Electrolux*, (where she mythologised her own early development); to evocative commentary, as in *The Gentle Art of Arranging Flowers*, to bold rhetoric, as in *What is to be our National Art?* In the process writings, another voice becomes clear, that of the experienced craft worker and educator, whose practicality was equal to adverse conditions, even those of wartime. Her repeated emphasis on improvisation regarding materials and techniques, gives valuable insights into her own art practice, as does her obvious dismay at the use of mechanical and formularised approaches to craft.

Certain devices occur repeatedly in the writing. A fondness for the apt metaphor, as when she compares the '*ironbound realism*' of Australian art to the newly opened '*Meccano*' Sydney Harbour Bridge, a love of paradox, evident in such statements as; '*An artist may work with a knowledge of science but he seldom works scientifically*'; bold declarations, such as '*There is nothing more horrible than realism in applied art*'; rhetorical questions, like '*Who wants Art?*'; and impassioned injunctions, such as '*Just get to it someone and originate.*' Mordant humour is also a weapon; '*For Applied Art, Apply to the Museum.*' All these contribute to the armoury of her expressions, helping to keep the work alive today, despite the sweeping nature of many of her statements. A composite picture emerges of an artist committed to developing an authentic approach to her artmaking and fiercely determined to encourage others to do the same.

Like many a returning traveler, Margaret MacPherson found the Australian art scene provincial and backward looking on her return home in 1919. She had been abroad, intermittently, for over a decade, studying in Europe and working, towards the end of the war, on soldier rehabilitation in England. By the time she returned she was over forty and set to marry William George Preston, recently discharged from the A.I.F. The couple married in Adelaide but settled in Sydney, which became the base for their peripatetic lifestyle. With newly acquired financial stability, it became possible for the artist to pursue a more independent line. As such, she advocated never making art with one eye on the market but, despite this assertion, it appears Preston was influenced by the market to some extent when her work did not sell and when public galleries did not acquire it.[5] Notwithstanding these provisos, she did, indeed, set out on three decades of artistic experimentation and created in the process some of the best loved images in Australian art.

During these years the couple travelled extensively, in Asia and the Pacific, China, Japan, Korea, the Americas, Europe, North Africa, India and the Middle East. Within Australia, they travelled to remote sites to experience Aboriginal and Torres Strait Islander art and rock carvings at first hand and to select art for exhibitions at home and abroad. Their destinations were challenging and adventurous, particularly when Preston's increasing age is considered, (she was nearing eighty when they travelled to North Africa and the Middle East). Even at home, they seemed unable to stay put, moving to various addresses in Mosman, Cremorne and Berowra.

The Sydney art scene in these years was a mixture of diverse personalities and forces, and prominent among them was Sydney Ure Smith. His roles as publisher of *Art in Australia,* proprietor of the commercial art studio, Smith & Julius, and President of the Sydney Society of Artists made him a valuable ally or opponent, depending on your allegiances. Although he decried cubism as 'a disease,' he championed Margaret Preston's work and consistently published her viewpoints and observations.

Some brief notes on the publications may help to context the work. *Art in Australia* and *The Home* (1920-1938) were both Sydney Ure Smith publications. The first was a high-quality quarterly that appeared between 1916 and 1942. In 1934 it was sold to Fairfax & Sons Ltd, with Ure Smith resigning as Editor in 1938. The journal continued until 1942, when war and changing perspectives saw its demise. It was reinvented by Sam Ure Smith, as *Art and Australia*, in 1963. However, after a change of ownership, in 2015, it was donated to the Victorian College of the Arts and, now called *Art + Australia*, it is a biannual digital publication.[6]

The Home, by far a more populist publication, was a magazine for women that echoed the style of sophisticated British journals. *Australia National Journal* (1939-1947) was a monthly, edited by Sydney Ure Smith and Gwen Morton Spencer. In addition to art and travel, its focus embraced architecture and industry and provided a forum for Ure Smith's interest in contemporary design. *The Sunday Pictorial* was the Sunday edition of the *Daily Telegraph Pictorial*, then owned by Associated Press. *Undergrowth* (1924-1929) was edited by former Julian Ashton students, Nancy Hall and Dore Hawthorne, and was published bimonthly. With an unprecedented focus on women artists and writers, the covers featured linocuts and woodcuts. *Manuscripts*, (1931-1935) was published and edited by Melbourne bookseller, Harry Tatlock Miller, later to be associated with Sydney's Merioola artists. The magazine had high production standards and was committed to contemporary art and letters, with John Tregenza noting that its outlook became progressively more avant-garde. Preston apparently liked the magazine's emphasis on linocuts, which were promoted as a modern democratic visual language. In *Manuscripts* she was in company with prominent Australian writers, artists and critics like George Bell, Leon Gellert and Harold Herbert.

As John Tregenza notes in his study of the years 1923-1954, nearly fifty Australian 'little magazines' appeared, few of which lasted more than four numbers.[7] Margaret Preston praised the efforts of all such publications in her 10th birthday message to the *Jindyworobak Review,* noting that the works of even short-lived magazines '*seem to cling to the most unexpected places and so the good work goes on.*' Both in the *Jindyworobak Review* and *Venture* (1937, 1939-40), Margaret Preston found a kindred spirit in editor and poet, Rex Ingamells. A Woiwurrung word, Jindyworobak meant 'to annex' or 'to join,' with Ingamells believing that a fusion of such words with his own language might express Australia's unique spirit of place. Rather more successfully, Margaret Preston was proposing a visual equivalent, using the language of Aboriginal and Torres Strait Islander design to express what was uniquely Australian.

Tregenza believes the small magazines were a way of combating cultural isolation as well as an attempt to define what was distinctively Australian. In that pre-television, pre-internet era, such magazines had an immediacy we associate with both, allowing a forum for new and dissenting voices, not found in the more established journals.

The focus of Margaret Preston's writings was relatively narrow. She did not deviate from her primary themes; the need for Australian artists to seek their own form of expression and the likelihood that inspiration could be found in Aboriginal and Torres Strait Islander art or the traditional arts of Asia and Japan. After World War 2, with the sense of urgency abating and people free to travel, some of the small magazines folded. As a result, Preston's writings increasingly appeared in the more established publications of Sydney Ure Smith.

There is a continuum in her support for the graphic qualities of Aboriginal and Torres Strait Islander art whose use of visual signs links to ideas of Synthetic Cubism, and the formalist theories of Roger Fry and others that she was exposed to in Europe. Cubism was divisive in this era when modern art was discussed, because of its ability to separate the progressive from the conservative. Modern European art had borrowed extensively from the 'primitive' and on her return home, Preston recognized the untapped power of Australia's own Aboriginal and Torres Strait Islander art. '*Totemism is one of the origins of art,*' she wrote in 1925, and '*it is ridiculous to deny that the aboriginal of Australia has no definite place in the making of a national art.*'

Again and again, she was to assert the modernist credo of rejecting '*downright realism*' and literary references in art. This emphasis contributed to some of her most contentious statements about Aboriginal and Torres Strait Islander art, such as; '*mythology and religious symbolism do not matter to the artist, only to the anthropologist.*' As much as the blind appropriation of another culture's imagery (a criticism frequently levelled at Preston), this could be seen as a rejection of the 'religious' sentiment that she despised in

Victorian art. She was to be uneasy with Surrealist literary references for similar reasons. Her attraction to 'oriental art' was also in keeping with modernist tenets, with Preston advocating the principle that art should not '*imitate nature as it is but in its ideal form.*' She wanted to create '*a purely Australian product*' and did not believe it could be achieved by the landscape traditions associated with the debate about a national art. Her vision was promoted internationally in 1941 with an exhibition at the Museum of Modern Art in New York (*Australia 1788-1941*).

Aspects of articles in this collection are repetitive but have been included to show the gradual evolution of Preston's ideas. Her cavalier attitude of the 1920s, advising the adoption of sacred patterns for cushion covers and golf socks, in time, was replaced by a more measured tone. By 1941, with first-hand experience of both the art and its creators, she could admit that she was '*humbly trying to follow them in an attempt to know the truth and paint it and so help to make a national art for Australia.*' Her repeated stress on the Aboriginal and Torres Strait Islander people as the '*lowest grade of humanity*' was generally followed by a denial, with their pictorial and decorative art cited as evidence to the contrary. '*The aborigine is an artist,*' she repeated, again and again; '*a true and sensitive artist whose work should be studied and treated with the respect that is due to true art.*'

Donna Leslie in her text on '*Margaret Preston and Assimilation*' notes that the anthropologist Frederick McCarthy, (a friend of Margaret Preston) continued to refer to the art as 'decorative'[8] even while he was interested in its meaning. Leslie asserts that rather than promoting the art in and for itself, Preston was advocating its appropriation in 'an art of assimilation' by white Australian artists to help distinguish Australian art from that of other countries. In this, Leslie argues, Preston was advocating for a cultural parallel to the policy of assimilation and also following in the footsteps of Paul Gauguin, whose Tahitian experience had helped to promote 'primitivism' in European art.

As Preston returned to other favoured themes (such as the role of American art in posing a warning or an inspiration) she sometimes made contradictory statements but the passage of the years brought new insights and she revised her opinions accordingly. Some views, particularly regarding the making of art, remained unchanged. She disliked facility in technique, a factor that influenced her questing mentality and her ability to change both medium and approach. The craft writings also reveal a hands-on, do-it-yourself mentality, the product of working under difficult conditions and the realization that artistic feeling is invariably stronger with '*the combination of the hand and the brain.*' Her rehabilitation work during World War 1 involved extensive improvisation, searching the moors for plants that would give dyes. Later she experimented with traditional Aboriginal colours, even bringing back sacks of sand, from her outback wanderings, to her Mosman hotel. Her changing living situations would also likely have contributed to her preferences for improvisation, along with a commitment to the smaller scale of works that such living conditions may have necessitated.

Her writing reflects this distrust of well-wrought style, jumping from one idea to another, in a lively, conversational manner. The transcript of her lecture at the Art Gallery of New South Wales in 1938 is a particular example of this and a curious insight into Preston's views on recent European contemporaries. Her advice to readers of *The Home* on how to decorate a bedroom provides another angle, particularly when contrasted with the electric candelabra and old Chinese ginger jars advised by other writers. As might be expected, Preston stresses an authentic minimalist approach, inclusive of the reader's own 'intimate possessions' and handicrafts.

Margaret Preston practised what she preached, at times becoming a semi-nomad who searched for inspiration in unlikely places. She was adept at finding her own masters, so she could learn from her own '*intuition how to understand them. No sitting down in Art Galleries or Art Schools, with Art served 'a la carte, nor any return to Australia with wonderful canvases of great successes.*' Over her long life, the young girl who aspired to the high stool in the art gallery, in *From Eggs to Electrolux*, became her own woman, and in the process made a unique and on-going contribution to Australian art.

ELIZABETH BUTEL

NOTES

1. Missingham, H. (1963) *Art and Australia*, Vol.1, No. 2, August 1963, p90.
2. Sayers, A. (2001) *Australian Art*, Oxford University Press.
3. Leslie, D. (2015) 'Margaret Preston and Assimilation', *Journal of Australian Indigenous Issues*, Volume 18, Issue 3, pp. 2-16.
4. Bowen, S. (1941) *Drawn From Life*, Collins, p22.
5. Butler, R. (1987) *The Prints of Margaret Preston: A Catalogue Raisonné*, Australian National Gallery, Melbourne Oxford University Press, p15.
6. Art + Australia. (2024). About Art + Australia. https://artandaustralia.com/profiles/art-and-australia
7. Tregenza, J. (1964) Australian Little Magazines 1923-1954, Libraries Board of South Australia, p64.
8. Leslie, D. (2015) 'Margaret Preston and Assimilation', *Journal of Australian Indigenous Issues*, Volume 18, Issue 3, p.5

Note : Spelling of place names in the travel articles has been updated and a small number of other corrections to spelling and punctuation have been made in line with current usage. Moreover in some texts Preston erroneously states views that have since been rejected. Similarly some names and titles mentioned in her articles are mistaken or incomplete.

A CONVERT TO MODERN ART

ART
IN AUSTRALIA
A QUARTERLY MAGAZINE

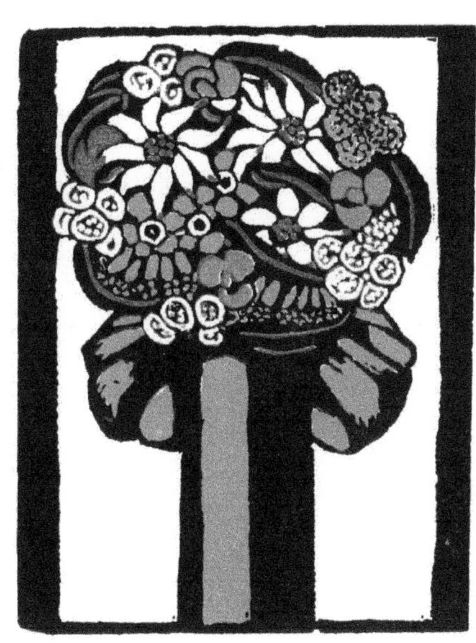

MARGARET PRESTON NUMBER

THIRD SERIES | DECEMBER, 1927 | NUMBER TWENTY-TWO

From Eggs To Electrolux

Art in Australia - Margaret Preston Number, 3rd Series, No. 22 December 1927

The woman whose work illustrates this book is alive. As a small girl of twelve years of age she was very much so, especially the day her mother took her to the National Gallery of Sydney to see the pictures there. She remembers quite well her excitement on going through the turnstile to be let at large in a big, quiet, nice-smelling place with a lot of pictures hanging on the walls and here and there students sitting on high stools copying at easels. Her first impression was not of the beauty or wonder of the pictures, but how nice it must be to sit on a high stool with admiring people giving you 'looks' as they went by, also she liked the smell of the place. She thinks now it must have been the kind of floor polish used on the linoleum.

This visit led her to decide to be an artist. Her mother being persuaded that she wasn't fit for anything else, asked advice from the schoolteacher, who recommended a needy friend. This friend gave tuition in an art that could be described as 'painting without tears', the process was so simple. A piece of frosted glass was placed over a copy of water lilies or swans, etc., and then pencilled through and afterwards coloured to copy.

One thing, however, the needy lady taught her, and that was to paint on china and bake the colours herself. There was a funny little gas oven in the backyard where the embryo artist experimented, so successfully, after a while, that at the mature age of thirteen she won a prize for china painting at a local show. This was a great feat, and was duly acknowledged by all her friends, but it wasn't sitting on a stool at the Art Gallery, so she started making enquiries as to the means of acquiring this honour. She found that the National Gallery authorities did not care for painting on frosted glass very much, that if she wanted to hang a work of hers on the walls and sit on a high stool it would be necessary to paint direct from Nature.

Then an inspiration came. As her mother knew no one who knew artists, why not go back to the Art Gallery and ask the man at the turnstile? He ought surely to know something, being with those pictures all day long. The idea was soon put into practice, and mother and daughter were presently interviewing the man of buttons. After some hesitation he wrote down the name of what he described as a 'nice promising young feller' who might teach. The artist's work, he said, was there in the Gallery and they could go and see it. At first sight it looked dreadful to them, but the artist-to-be explained to her mother that she had heard of the 'Broad' school, so it must be that kind, but they took the addresses of two other artists whose work met all their requirements in detail and subject. These two artists declined teaching young buds to sprout, so her mother took her to the 'promising young feller', who was very nice and helpful and promised that everything she did was to be from life. Her first still life was begun in a studio in Angel Place. History has no memory of it, but a picture of a striped tablecloth with a studio pot hung for many years in the attic room of our young friend.

After some months of careful teaching, the promising young man, W. Lister Lister, who was really a very thoughtful person, suggested that it would be wiser if she were sent to Melbourne to learn, in a big school with other students, how to draw from the antique, to begin from the beginning. As it made no difference to her family where they lived - her father being on the sea - they went to Melbourne.

Some little time before this, the Victorian National Gallery had acquired a new master, and his fame was immense. It was to this great man she was sent.

She began her drawing lessons at this school with one of the kindest, cleverest artists Australia has produced, Fred McCubbin. He has gone now, but the memory of that nice man always remains. He really didn't teach. The students would wait their turn for a lesson, but when he came it was generally only to hear that still more could be done. He gave nothing constructive. In spite of this, he was the best teacher she could have had, as it allowed her to feel that there was someone to help but not to influence.

Life did not go on in this peaceful way all the time, for at intervals the new master would unexpectedly appear, Bernard Hall. Austere, biting, and immaculate, he generally left bowed spirits in his wake, also intense admiration.

At various times in the year this new master demanded that victims of a certain standard in drawing should be laid on the altar of paint under his supervision. So, after a time spent in acquiring drawing prizes, the message came that our friend was ready for higher instruction. The teaching was magnificent; after the gentle little man in the drawing school it came as a revelation. He was certainly the finest teacher she ever had; every student respected and feared him. Slender, well built, with stiff cropped head and sallow face, always faultlessly groomed even to enter the teaching studios, this man set an example to young Australia that those who came under his influence at that time have never forgotten. But wasn't he vitriolic! Nerves of iron and talent were necessary to stand his onslaughts, especially to one who could not appreciate his liking for hideous models.

Fate intervened to help our little friend. It was necessary to draw numbers to get a place at the model, and as she always seemed to draw last, and therefore worst place, she was allowed, because of the crowded classes, to work quietly at still life in the adjoining studio. Here she would work day in and day out at her precious eggs, etc. Often many days would she spend painting at a small high light, such perfection of detail being demanded. Her fortune sometimes deserted her, and back she would have to go to the human figure - drawing for so long that she never seemed to have time to begin in colour.

Again she wins a drawing prize, but the next year was a happy one, for the still life scholarship was hers. It would seem that a liking for the colour and form of inanimate objects was born in her.

Then comes a domestic upset, and she finds it necessary to go with her family to Adelaide, there to teach for a year or so and then return to Melbourne for fresh instruction. This stay at the Melbourne Gallery was only a short one, as it was imperative that she should return to Adelaide to continue with her teaching.

Her art work was really begun at this time. It shows a movement of thought which is continuous throughout. As a young girl, not yet in her twenties, she made up her mind to teach for her living and paint her pictures as she would, to choose her own subjects and do them in her own way, leaving all thought of selling out of her mind. From Monday morning until Saturday she taught. Fortunately, her pupils were pleasant, so that her nerves were not racked when she started on her own work at the weekends.

Against all opposition of friends and relatives she painted eggs, dead rabbits, onions - just everything she liked. It was no use for her to explain to people that the standardised beauty for art of landscapes, sunsets and ladies did not interest her; that as she felt no pleasure in them, how could she possibly say anything in pencil or paint that would interest anybody else? So she simply didn't try. Every weekend found her painting away at her eggs or rabbits; her ideal at this time was to paint them with such fidelity to nature that they could almost be used in the kitchen.

As soon as she saw her hopes likely to be realised, her mind worried her. If she really painted as well as that, surely she would be the very best painter of still life in the world. The doing of it was so easy. It was this fact that raised a doubt in her mind about her possible fame; so being orphaned, she started to put by pence until they became pounds, to take a trip abroad to see really where she stood and also to get some 'finishing' lessons.

A specimen of her work at this time is 'Eggs', now belonging to the Royal Art Society. It was bought from the annual Art Society's Exhibition for five pounds, a price considered outrageously high for such common objects.

The pence had now become sufficient pounds to take the wonderful trip abroad. She starts off with a friend intending to live in Munich for some two years. Paris was not chosen, as the French reputation did not come up to the desired standard of her friend's parent, so they went Germany-wards. Her art tour began in Venice, but as nothing impresses the ignorant, Titian and his fellow artists roused little enthusiasm in her mind - in fact, her feeling was one of sympathy with an irate American lady whom she heard saying in a loud voice to her husband as they strode through a Belgian Gallery: 'Rubbens - Rubbens; if I see any more of that man's paint I'll go mad'.

It took Munich and the Secessionists to awaken her. In the beginning she hated the big Government Art School for Women; having her lessons translated to her drove her frantic. She simply couldn't understand. There in that horrid country no one seemed to understand Australian German, or appreciate Australian art. They were all hopeless. It was even worse for her when she found herself understanding in German what apparently sane artists and students were saying about a certain picture at a Secessionist Exhibition - a picture that had a large pink dragon, with a lady victim clad in yellow, being rescued by a gentleman in black clothes, not armour - clothes! They were actually admiring it. It made her feel sick. She much preferred the good old art show then on at the same time, where lemons were fruit and dragons standardized lizards. In fact, the only art she really admired in Munich was Durer's painting of two apostles, one having a whole landscape painted on the pupil of his eye. This to her was Art. Things were so bad that a decision had to be made; she couldn't stay in a country going mad; so in spite of the possible upset to her friend's morals, she would go to Paris.

It was a freezing morning when she left Munich. Snow lay thick everywhere. It was a regular Napoleon's march from Moscow, both having Paris for their objective. Once settled in Paris she started to feel the air, by visiting the exhibitions then open. Alas! for all her hopes. The Autumn Salon was just closing, but she found this show exceeded the outrageousness of the Secessionists. Under these distressing conditions there was only one thing to be done - to get a teacher who was a moderate and yet intelligent, to explain and teach what these people thought they were doing.

The first thing that wise man did was to realise that our little Australian was really worried and wanted to learn. So he sent her to study Japanese art at the Guimet Musee, to let her learn slowly that there is more than one vision in art. That a picture could have more than eye realism. That there was such a thing as aesthetic feeling. That a picture that is meant to fill a certain space should decorate that space. That the time of Giotto had passed when he painted to teach. Nowadays, books and education were being given away. That each century should have some of the characteristics of itself in its art. All this and so much more that our poor little artist was obliged to become a very humble student indeed.

She found she had been hopping about on one rung only of the ladder of art. Starting off again she tries to add another quality to her realism - that of decoration. Hunting the galleries of Spain, Holland and Italy, etc., she has learnt to appreciate the mighty qualities in the works in these countries. But it all costs so much money that she finds that her pounds have become pence, so it was necessary to return to Adelaide to teach and earn.

Her work at this period shows a definite move from sheer realism - the 'Onions' in the National Gallery, Adelaide, and 'Roses' owned by the Broken Hill Gallery were painted at this time.

On her return to Adelaide, she started teaching and working at her picture-making, trying to find her feet for her new movement - the addition of design in colour to realism. But now how difficult are friends and relatives, and so inconsistent. Only a few years ago they were grumbling because she would paint such horrid subjects as dead rabbits and fresh eggs. Now they were complaining because she is painting large gay flowers against gay backgrounds. 'Oh, why will you do it,' they say, 'when you had begun to sell and were getting on so nicely with those dark mysterious backgrounds and quiet material?'

As she had no desire to sell unwanted work, she was quite free to pursue her own destiny. Back in Adelaide once more, how she craved for just one glimpse of that pink dragon. She felt that her knowledge was so small, but she knew that no one could help her but herself, so there was nothing to do but plod on, work out on canvas that which bothered her mind. For two years she experimented in colour, searching always to get an aesthetic feeling in her work, and all the time penny-piling to be able to make a dash back to Paris to see if she had moved a little. The collection for the trip this time went quicker, as being older and more experienced she received more students, so that by the end of two years she was able to return to Paris to refresh herself. Her work from this time onwards is based on colour principles. She developed a scale of colour to suit herself, and with the combination of realism produced such work as 'Anemones'.

A year in Paris and she then left that city to live in London. Her first exhibit was at the Academy, where she was reported as a colourist. This let her definitely know the move had been made. Solitary realism lay at the back with her adolescence. From now on she allowed herself full license in colour - only letting her subjects appear as realistic as her aesthetic feelings allowed.

Exhibiting and teaching, she found her days full, when crash, down came the war. She decided to try and help mend soldiers, as she had no capacities to heal, and so went to a pottery school and learnt simple rules of that trade. She had as a teacher one who did throwing of shapes on the wheel for Doulton's, so her good fortune in teachers still stood by her. After a time she was able to teach shell-shocked men simple pottery. Down on the Devon Moors she worked with them until the armistice came and she was free to come home. There are two nice pots in the London War Museum made under her tuition by shell-shocked soldiers.

Returning again to Australia, she took on domestic duties, finding time to continue with her art. Still painting in colour with a set principle in her mind, she produced 'Apples', 'Thea Proctor's Tea Party', and 'Hibiscus. Yet again the old restless feeling is bothering her. She feels that her art does not suit the times, that her mentality has changed and that her work is not following her mind. She feels that this is a mechanical age - a scientific one - highly civilized and unaesthetic. She knows that the time has come to express her surroundings in her work. All around her in the simple domestic life is machinery - patent ice-chests that need no ice, machinery does it; irons heated by invisible heat; washing-up machines; electric sweepers, and so on. They all surround her and influence her mind and, as her mind is expressed in her work, she has produced 'Still Life, 1927', and 'Banksias'.

Yet again come her friends and critics. Queer people. Only a short time since they were complaining that her colour knocked everything out, and now that she is trying to produce form in its simplest manner, making all other qualities subservient to this, they regret her throwing away of her 'beautiful colour'. Fortunately she is free to paint what she pleases and how she thinks. She does not imagine she has advanced in her art - only moved. The ladder of art lies flat, not vertical. This only she claims for the works in this book. They are the mind of a woman who is still alive.

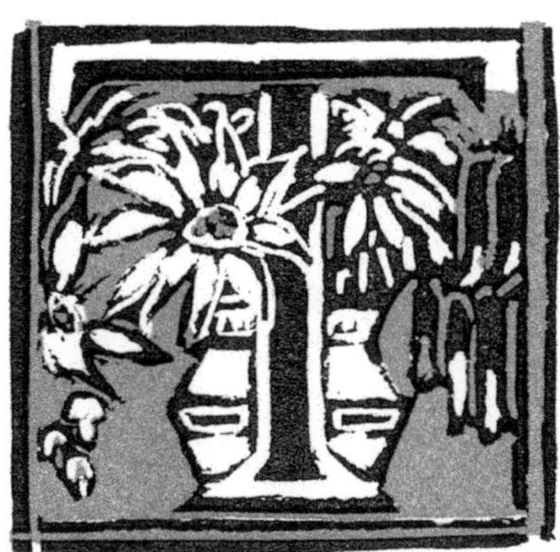

Initial 'T' woodblock print by Preston, size unknown, *Art in Australia*, December 1927.

Why I Became a Convert to Modern Art

The Home Vol. 4, No. 2. June 1923

The Character of an Individual is not a fixed property.
T. S. Eliot

Once upon a time when I was twelve years of age I borrowed my mother's best dinner plates and brunswick blacked them all over. On to the blacking I painted flannel flowers. The result so impressed my mother that after the shock of the loss of the plates was over she determined to have me properly trained. Her justification was that as the flowers were the image of the natural ones I must have talent.

From this on my imitativeness was well nurtured.

Excellent tuition was found for me, and I was well taught to draw the outward show of dancing fauns, Donatello heads, etc. I was well surrounded by tradition and taught only through tradition. Would that I could have had the advantages offered by the Slade school in London, where the sculpture of the Greeks & Co. flourish in museums and not in a live school, and where all imitativeness is discouraged. I must have learnt to draw, for I won so many prizes. After some years of this excellent training I was allowed to start on colour. Oranges, turnips, bald heads, hairy heads, bananas, etc., all were imaged by me, and more prizes followed.

At last 1 felt competent to face the future, let it be eggs, onions or portraits.

I had been magnificently grounded, and all I had to do was to go on doing more, as I had nature always before me and how could anyone improve on Nature? What is a plate but a dish and an onion but a vegetable?

Then full steam ahead in art.

As long as the onions were of a recognised species, and plates as they are generally known, all was well. Trees and portraits with a little gentle selection were equally safe so long as you were careful to arrange the lights according to nature. This was the text-book of my early realism. Imitating the world, I decided to go abroad, and fixed on Munich.

There were two very strong elements in Munich at that time, the dead realists and the lively moderns. These two sets of painters had their shows at the same time. Naturally, I condemned as mad and vicious the moderns and went willingly with the deads. 1 was well soaked in 'nature above all' and 'sanity first' and the boat fare afterwards. My first visit to the Secession Exhibition, as the modern show called itself, left me undefiled.

To the pure all is pure, to the blank all is blank.

My letters about this time written back to my native country could be compressed into a few sentences such as: *Half German art is mad and vicious and a good deal of it is dull; I am glad to say my work stands with the best of them.*

Six months after another tabloid letter could have been received: You were astonished when you read that I am starting to think that perhaps the mad and vicious show has something in it.

And again: *I have found out one thing from them - that eggs don't need to be peculiarly Wyandotte, etc., and they can still be eggs.*

This discovery gave me bad growing pains.

I suffered all the discomforts of doubt and indecision and, much worried, determined to leave Germany and go to Paris. When I arrived in Paris the Old Salon (francaise) was open.

Here I found realism triumphant!

Myriads of canvases!

It seemed as if all the artists in the world must be showing there.

But again, its very multitudinousness made me think that if painting is as easy as this, why is it regarded as an art? So again I paid my door money to a modern show and this time tried to think.

I found at last that the eggs and onions as part or whole of a picture could appear different and suggest something more than being merely edible. I could not paint the smell so I needn't paint the species. Realism had its first rebuff.

I went to the Galleries and studied Ingres and Renoir, etc., and so, muddled and worried, I moved on to Spain to worship at the shrine of Velasquez, that demi-god of realism. Velasquez occupied a large room, but, alas, so did Goya. Like the Wandering Jew 1 fled from country to country hunting an ideal, and finally decided to come back to Australia. I had learned to think - so the passage money was not wasted. Australia is a fine place in which to think.

The galleries are so well fenced in.

The theatres and cinemas are so well fenced in.

The libraries are so well fenced in.

The universities are so well fenced in.

You do not get bothered with foolish new ideas. Tradition thinks for you, but Heavens! how dull! To keep myself from pouring out the selfsame pictures every year I started to think things out.

Why is music so controlled and painting such a muddle? Because music is a science and painting is uncontrolled. How can art be controlled? By a scientific study of optics, etc.

When does an onion cease to become a kitchen requisite and useful to art? When the onion becomes merely an aesthetic object for the painter?

What is the difference between an onion in art and one in commerce? In art we must use nature as tradition only and originate another suggestion apart from food and fecundity.

Why does the tobacco-juice art (Vandyck brown) flourish in Australia in preference to the light and colour sect? Because the appreciation of colour was nearly killed in the Victorian era, and most of the art here has not emerged from that period.

When is a work modern? When it represents the age it is painted in.

These answers were my revised text-book. And so I started to try not to duplicate nature, but to endeavour to make my onions, etc., obey me, and not me them. To add my mind (aestheticism) to their contours and let my eyes be more controlled by my brain. And now 1 want to think and think and try and get those onions, etc., without any remembrance of the Greek, German, French brand, and portray them as a purely Australian product.

It's going to be difficult, but anything is better than turning a handle and finding myself doing brunswick blacked dinner plates, only a little more fluently.

Australian Artists Versus Art

Art in Australia 3rd series, No. 26. December 1928

This is an age of technical expertness, commercialism and imitativeness! Science reigns supreme. But starry-eyed Science hangs on an If - so that her day must be short. The country that produces only Robots is unimportant. Anything that has a formula is useless as a means of making a country great, or of producing something that is not secondary. An artist must be spontaneous, therefore, every country is dependent on its artists to uphold its name and place it among the 'Great' of the world. Old lands, old heads, old traditions are all excellent in their own places, but they are the very devil when they try to usurp 'the right to think' and the habits of others than those to which they have themselves been accustomed. Australia is at present complacently sitting on a stool declaring that her youth is preventing her from doing anything. It is, 'Wait until we are older and then you will see - at present we are so young.' Not so young, dear Australia, but that unless some bright young students settle down to try, to originate, to think, and to ignore their Cook's tourist experience in the galleries and schools of old countries, Australia will be simply a replica of America, who has deluged herself with the works of dead and alive artists of other lands; so much so that she has now no possibility for centuries of producing any art that is not reminiscent of another country.

One great trouble in this young country is that there is a certain diffidence in the Australian mind as to whether, owing to its extreme youth and distance from Grandpa G Britain, it is possible to produce anything as good as is done by those important people. The old heads are not troubled in this fashion, they do not believe in any work but that which they produce. Australia is swamped with it, but, alas, it is work reminiscent of their own separate countries or their teachers, who must have been imported, as Captain Cook only called on Australia something over a hundred years ago. They naturally think that such art is 'Australian' because it is of an Australian subject, painted by an Australian and in Australia; does it not occur to them how very similar is this 'Australian' picture to those of other countries? The mountains may be smaller or the skies bluer, but let them examine the picture intelligently, and, apart from such immaterial things, they will find their Australian art very much 'School' of.

The trouble lies partly with the connoisseur and partly with the artist. The art critic does not demand anything more (except in a very few cases) than what he has offered to him and, in fact, the more like to that to which he is accustomed the better he thinks the picture. The artist as yet does not seem to be prepared 'mentally' to do his job, but now comes the younger generation, demanding the right to their country, to an expression in their own methods and disliking apron strings. What are their abilities? When the student has had all the technical instruction he can get, he seems to think it time to get the cash back as quickly as possible; he does not stop to think of his enormous luck in being in this young country, and that he should study its topographical features, so distinct in their character from other countries; the characteristic aspects of a nature that has produced the aboriginal, kangaroo and platypus, to know the difference of the growth of an oak to a she-oak, etc., in fact to work hard with constructive brains before he dashes into picture or the making of any of the Arts.

Who has attempted to study the spiritual side of this great land? And who, again, has studied 'form' from literature? How many young Australian artists have studied 'form' from the Bible? Stanley Spencer has done so and London and the Continent proclaim him one of the finest and most original of living artists. And then, why not study some of Roger Fry's essays? 'Plastic Colour' for instance. The study of literature, if it does affect the student at all, must be of advantage, because there is no optic vision, therefore no copying by unconscious memory. A study of the difference in English and Continental literature helps to teach that each nation has its own character. Art cannot be turned into Esperanto, so that when the student discovers for himself the 'spiritual' differences in these countries, then let this young Australian paint his subject; but without the knowledge of this difference Art will never be born in Australia.

Here are a few art laws of the Chinese, whose art is so wonderfully distinctive:

1. Cultivate a full and catholic spirit.
2. Observe wisely and comprehensively.
3. Take in the essentials of the scene and discard trivialities.
4. Have a varied and extensive experience.

In brief, the necessity of objectivity is urged, but, at the same time, the importance of subjective expression is emphasised. Until the brain works in conjunction with the spiritual vision, Australian artists will never produce anything different from that work produced in the studios where they learn their trade. After all is said and done, Art is, aesthetically speaking, but a product of the imagination and should be worked with and enjoyed by the same faculty.

The hopes for an Australian Art at present are good; some of the younger group are personal, some believe in the Esperanto of Art, and others work out their own ideas - the promising thing is that these younger people are starting to think for themselves. The old order will go (as it did in Greece) when the artist is also student - then the Robots will be put in their proper places - mechanical instructors of the mechanical part of Art, but when finished with, put in the 'box room'. Australia is young, admittedly, but youth is the time for experiment. The lack of money, to be able to spend years 'searching' before any actual 'profit' can be made, may be urged by the average student. Go and do something else and do Art as did Henri Rousseau, 'le douanier'. Do not turn the one religion that is born in everybody's body (diseased excepted), that of an ideal, into 'good press reports'. Art is an ideal, it is mind before matter. The Robot in Art makes 'The Man in the Street' his equal. The student artist makes 'The Man to Think' and this is the only way that a public can be educated and Australia's name be amongst the great.

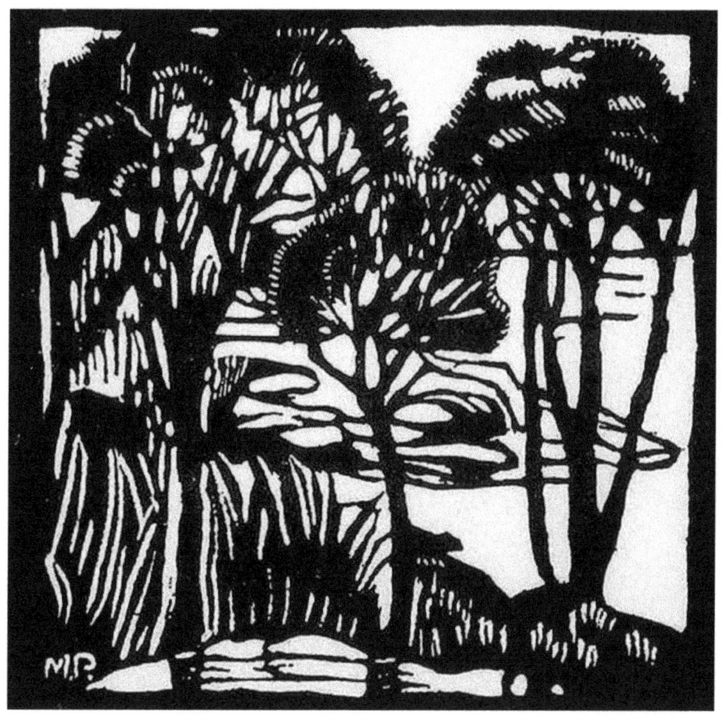

'Tea-Tree' woodblock by Preston c.1929, from *Margaret Preston Recent Paintings* (Ure Smith, 1929).

Meccano as an Ideal

Manuscripts No 2 June 1932

Sydney, New South Wales, has built for itself some of the finest specimens of Meccano art in the world. One, a great towering structure that sends everything around it out of perspective; it is the adored of three parts of the community - it is 'Our Bridge'. In an odd way, it seems to be the culmination of the worship of ironbound realism that has ruled the art of Australia generally. Repetition and diligence is the order of the Meccano.

Number two specimen is a new fountain which has been placed in Sydney's principal public reserve - Hyde Park. It is a veritable repetition of all the public fountains in the world. All the laws of fountains have been obeyed in its figures: they lean, they stride, they invite criticism as to what gods they represent. They follow in perfect order in the repetition of an idea born about the time of the fig-leaf era. It is a perfect specimen of Meccano art.

The third erection is the cenotaph. This was once a distinguished-looking mausoleum of marble, simple in line, stern in its simplicity. These qualities gave offence, and now two useless-looking soldier figures have been added - a pair, one at each end of the slab. Every rag, button, etc. true to a soldier's kit; all in order, realism without offering conviction of grief or anything else but tailors' dummies. The cenotaph has joined the great union of Meccano.

This god, Meccano, rules this country with a rod. It demands all landscape paintings to be on a set pattern, or no Wynne or other prize - all portraits to be after set laws and rules, or no Archibald prize - a National Art out of a box, easy to do, to understand, and - to ignore!

'Who wants Art', says the man in the street. Here, in a country geographically and climatically different to any other country, and with its own national characteristics, an imported toy is its ideal.

While the Meccano god rules, Australian art can have no hope, as an artist may work with a knowledge of science, but he seldom works scientifically, by laws and rules. He works through his artistic vision and conception.

Art is personal, and of the spirit - both of these are anathema to the god Meccano. Let young Australia rise and smash this footling god, and demand that work showing their national characteristics can be exhibited without jeers from press reporters and aged committee men. Let young Australia have growing pains, remembering that all the outraged bellowings of the god Meccano can never stop growth. Have courage, before it is too late, before this country is poisoned by internationalism, making its art bastard forever.

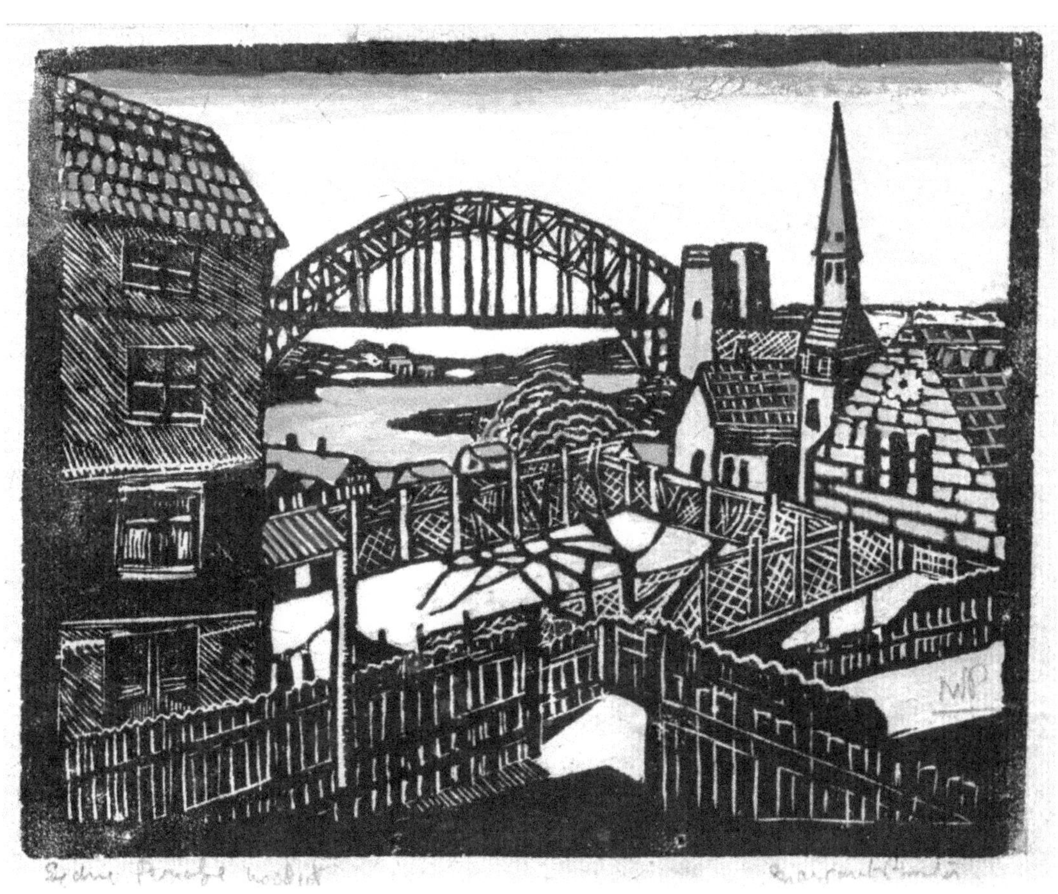

'The Bridge from the North Shore', woodblock print c. 1932, 19.1 x 23.2 cm.

An Exhibition, 1933

Manuscripts, No. 4. February 1933

It is proposed that an exhibition of modern pictures be shown in Australia about March, 1933. It is to be a collection of the works of artists who are original thinkers, who feel and show that birth is better than rebirth, that the mind must rule the eye.

The names of some of the artists are amongst the world's finest painters: Picasso, John, Nash, Ethelbert White, Gauguin, are but a few, and before their arrival in this continent it might help a little to point out a few reasons why they should be accepted in Australia from the Antipodean standpoint, and not judged as harmless maniacs with an eye to notoriety.

The painter who is acknowledged to be about the world's finest artist at the present is Picasso. This painter has shown work from time to time in different stages of his mentality. His first era was of the kind called by academicians - the perfect draughtsmanship type. It was never vulgarly realistic, but understandable to the ordinary eye. In his next era he gave to the world the finest cubist work it has ever seen. In this he dispensed with 'contour'. He belonged to the movement that believed as the architect is formal in his design so could plastic art achieve artistic results without representing objects and things. The following are some of the fundamental ideas of cubism:

1. To have a definite geometrical axis.
2. To use perspective as a servant, not as a master. In other words, to use it when and where it is needed, so that if distortion is necessary to the work it can be used equally as the set rules of perspective.
3. To give objects geometrical shapes in formal relation to each other.
4. To absolutely eliminate all photographic likeness and return to classical form (Michelangelo).

It is a revulsion against the anecdotal type of art - so much better done in literature as pleasant uplifting work - such as Denby Sadler's 'To the King.' Luke Filde's 'The Doctor,' Bourgereau's 'Madonna and Child,' and Peter Graham's 'Sheep in Mist.' The reason for the explanation of a few of the cubist ideals is because cubism is the foundation of all the twentieth century thoughtful original work. In the third era of

Picasso he used his knowledge gained from cubism with his wonderful draughtsmanship. In doing so he added to his austerity, directness of line and massiveness of form. His colour he kept subservient, so that his work at this period suggests the dignity of cathedrals, resulting in pure aesthetic art. His last work is a fantasy in cubism. Eliminating all ordinary form, he has apparently been influenced by the heritage of his birth. He is an Andalusian, a descendant of Arabs, and now seems to have returned to the traditions of his race, to an abstract art based on the Arabesque. He appears to have thrown his mind back to his childhood days, so that the forms which he now expresses will contain no humanity, or allow of any human emotion. The illustration included is from one of his latest works, and is in the return to the Arabesque mood. This work has been done by a man who has seriously been compared to Michelangelo.

Then there is Augustus John, England's greatest portrait painter. He is easier to appreciate, because where Picasso is classical, John is a Romantic. By these terms is meant, John is a Romanticist because he expressed human attributes such as power, pride, etc., but Picasso subjects all these to pure form. In his portraits, John gives the mentality and importance of his sitter. One, of Lloyd George, painted during the early part of the war, had the head a size and a half larger than life. It gave the feeling to the spectator of a being who lived in a big world and was part of it. The colour was insignificant to the features and forms; thus, not detracting by 'life likeness', it gave a force to the subject. An ordinary life size portrait of Lloyd George tinkered with every hair in the head and moustache, with all the little wrinkles put in and the pinky-white skin well emphasised, would have pleased the popular idea, but would have given no idea of the capabilities of the sitter. It could have been a mere mask that a coloured photograph could have done much better. The greatest good that scientists can do for artists is to discover colour photography. It will do away with the Imitatives, and put the science of painting in a position it can never hold until this happens.

Nash and Ethelbert White are also English painters. One could suspect John of Irish blood, but never these two artists. They are more individual than original, they are therefore again the more easily understood. Something, never seen before, with no human appeal is difficult to accept, but something that has individual qualities appearing more human is easier. This is why realistic work is so popular. It is what everyone sees and knows, and it is done over and over again, but by this fact is doomed by reason of over production. The works of Nash and White are strongly placed on geometrical rules, nothing is left to chance. A sunny cornfield by Nash is presented in perfect forms and friendly colour, no shape has been littered with useless detail, and yet so excellent are the sizes and forms that there is no suggestion of vacancy. Some trees in a field by Ethelbert White might annoy by reason of the tops of the trees being drawn to one point and the colour being a dun brown only - if the eye is worried about things like these, let the mind help. Take the forms of the foliage piece by piece and see how reasonable, how guided, they all are until they all form one big shape. Compare them with some of the work of the cheap realistic artists having the trees with their foliage scampering all over the canvas - remember that 'Art' is placing in a set size something that will delight the mind before the eye. To the painter nature cannot be captured or tamed, she can only be translated. Gauguin, who is also to be represented, was a Frenchman whose work has been so reproduced that the first shock of his originality is now well over. He also is a Romanticist, owing a lot to his devotion to colour, and colour that he places so scientifically, even to putting a vermilion dog in a landscape where it was necessary as a complementary in colour to his work. His love of beautiful designs and colour may not have allowed him to be one of the great masters, as any human attribute detracts from the gods, but it certainly has allowed him a place very near them. It is admitted that his figures are not the surf models of the press and the academies, but they are always part of the whole of his picture, not one spot of these colours called man, woman, or child can be done without.

In cool opposition there will be the work of Wadsworth - a great cubist also. His still life is the most modern of the present day, regulated like machines in colour, form, and design, giving the appearance of abject reality, but as you love realism, beware. This work is no mere imagery, but is calculated to its last geometrical line.

The simplest way then for the layman to understand the real moderns is to grasp these few facts. Geometry is the base of their work. These painters have a definite revulsion against photographic realism in technique or in any way that paint is expressed. It is necessary to admit that the artist has as much right to a point of view as a scientist and that, to cultivate an aesthetic quality of criticism, the critic should look at these modern works not once only, but look and think long enough to definitely make up the mind whether it can, cannot, or if it even wishes to understand what the painter has said.

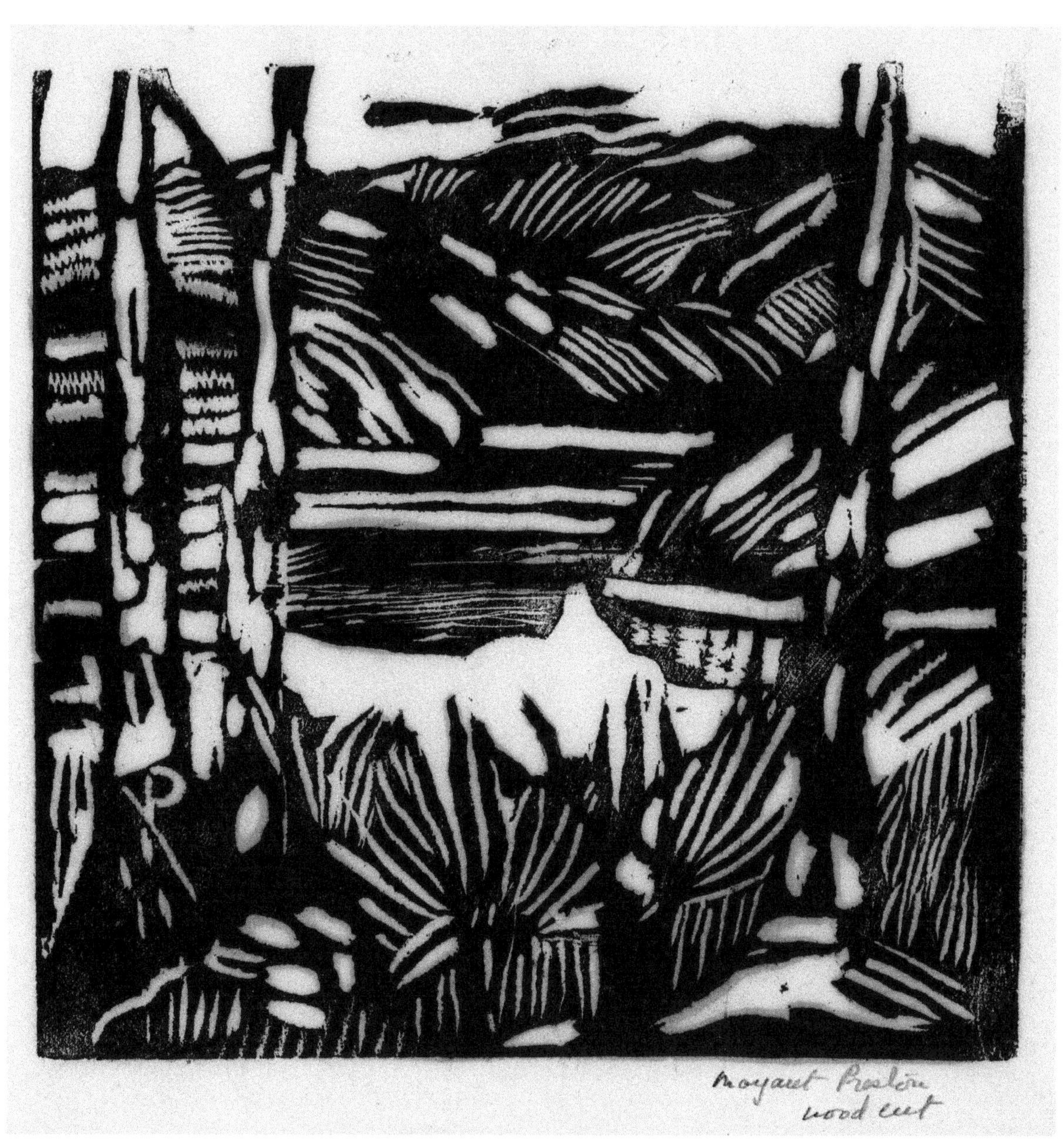

'Calabash Bay, Berowra', woodblock print c. 1938, 19.1 x 18.8 cm.

The Moderns to this year 1938

Art in Australia 3rd Series, No 72, 1938

In the last lecture we left Matisse as a link between the Impressionists and the Art of today. It is difficult to explain Modern Art as there is no perspective from which to judge it. It is necessary to know that an artist is influenced by the social conditions surrounding him. If this is not so he is either a very strong individualist or merely a craftsman. This is an age which has robbed us of humanity, morals and control. It is an age of science and speed, it is chaotic and sensationalism is a part of public life and is not reserved for the individual alone. All this shows in the work of the artist. It has become scientific, nostalgic, nightmarish and fantastical.

The foundation of many modern movements is Abstract Art. This is an Art in which the natural forms of nature such as the cube, circle and square of geometry take the place of the natural object. For instance a face is reduced to its outward form, which is an oval. This shape, if it is to be the dominant note or theme, is repeated in the planes that the artist needs for the building of his picture.

As it is not possible to go through all the art movements of today, the three principal groups will be discussed. They are the Cubists, the Neo Romanticists and the Surrealists. After these we will get a glimpse at the art of tomorrow with its architectural tendencies very strongly in evidence. Starting with Cubism, which came very shortly after a small group of artists who called themselves Crystallographers, Frank Rutter tells how this movement began. It was through a painter who went with a student friend to a science lecture on mineralogy at the Sorbonne in Paris. He came back with his head seething over the fact that the crystal in nature is the base of a certain geometrical form. It is six-sided and in the shape of a cube. The artist deduced from this that all secondary' shapes such as arcs, circles and others came from the reduction of the curves and edges of the first shape. It was from these facts that Cubism sprang and the Crystallographers got their name. The idea is not new as in some of Durer's drawings the heads have been strengthened by this method and it can be seen in some old Persian manuscripts. Prior to Cubism it was Cezanne who said that nature could be expressed by the cube, the cone and the cylinder.

What exactly is Cubism? It is the pure form of Geometry. The Cubist relies solely on his straight lines, curves, surface and solid forms for his interest; he has no pretty faces or smiling landscapes to help him, he has only sheer hard architectural forms. Cubism in no way represents the object. The great thing about this phase of art is that all pictures painted in this way must be built and not put on the canvas thoughtlessly. This movement had some very strong painters such as Picasso, Braque and Leger who were at its head. At the beginning Braque showed landscapes and seascapes with the waves like razor edges, Picasso was doing the same thing with the human form. These were patterns of shapes with colours that had nothing to do with the natural figure.

Braque and Leger have stood firmly by Cubism, especially Leger whose work has not allowed even colour to interfere with it. Picasso, who is a Spanish Jew, has since gone into many more movements. As he stands at the head of modern art today it is interesting to follow his work. First he was almost a realist, then he painted portraits; this was when he was under the influence of Toulouse Lautrec. Another period followed when he painted meagre nudes and harlequins; these seem to be the result of a study of Ingres. Later he became an ardent Cubist after he had investigated its formula of simple forms. It was not long before he developed another way to work. This was by superimposing his forms one on the other, so that the side, back and front of the face showed at the same time. These are really works of ingenuity and as they are built plane on plane they are artistic mathematical tables. From these experiments he left Cubism and painted some magnificent portraits, one of his wife that is particularly fine. This phase did not last long and soon he entered a world of his own composing, by taking a subject, dissecting it and recomposing and moulding it into different shapes. He has done this with his colour as well. Now he has entered a world of monsters of his own brain. Picasso originates forms that have never been in existence yet are full of artistic necessity and are, in the correctness of their construction, capable of Being. This artist's work is that of creation and in these last works of inhuman grotesques, he has left behind him the cold intellectuality of his cubist work and struck out for an artistic emotionalism. The great failure of his work is its utter lack of humanity.

Discussing yet further, the reason why he has had such an important influence on this age, is that he has never imitated but always created; for instance in his invention of non-existent objects, he has done so from the knowledge that there are three kinds of forms. There is the crude original form of nature, then there is the form elaborated by geometry, and thirdly the forms made by art. Picasso has succeeded in the third form and has now taken to the dreams and distortions of Surrealism. For the moment he has given up pictorial art and is writing poetry; his companion Braque has stayed a cubist but has added lovely colour to his Designs. These are always in perfect symmetry. He thinks only in terms of colour and form. His work, which is generally based on still life, is very architectural in its structure.

Leger is the true Cubist of the three. His work is pure automatism. His colour is suitable to his forms and suggests the simplicity of the early primitives in the use of simple masses of primary colours. Whereas in the work of Braque, the colours blend with each other, in that of Leger, colour is only necessary to the subject. This automatism is the principle of his imagination; he is only interested in form and its aspects. His theme is the cylinder, and he has used it in so many of his compositions that he has almost become the patron saint of motor cars, airplanes and streamline trains. Leger has written a book on contemporary art and is the head of a big art school.

The next movement that followed Cubism was short lived but it was a most important one for two reasons. It was a break away from intellectualism to emotionalism and it also produced some of the most brilliant young men of our time. The movement was called the Neo Romanticists. This idea was a strong protest against the machinelike Cubism and aimed at representing Poesy. The first paintings were made dim and mysterious and were generally painted in a deep blue, which gave them a look of sadness and mystery. These artists, unlike the cubists, painted the human face and body but their images were thoughtful and were shown in a complicated manner as befits the modern mind. Man as they painted him was a complex and melancholy being. This is why they painted him against a broken column or under a thick blanket of snow or covering, as they wished to show that he was a depressed being full of despair and nostalgia. The finest painters of this group are Berard, and Leonid Berman.

Berard has painted at least one picture that is a masterpiece. It is a dual self portrait. There are two heads in the picture but only (one) body is shown, the other is behind the first, which is the figure of a man in a bath robe sitting on a sandy beach, with a background that does not seem to be connected with the figures in front. It looks extraordinarily simple but is subtle in the extreme, both in colour and design. The next movement to follow was Surrealism, this is pure Psychic automatism, it has neither reason, moral or aesthetic preoccupation and is 'thinking' in paint. It is really fancy divorced from reason.

Surrealism is not a new idea, it goes back to any century. By its nature, art is illusionistic, so that when Fantasy goes wild and becomes diabolical we get such work as that of Hieronymus Bosch of the 15th Century, that author of nightmare. With him, fantasy becomes demoniacal. He represented the troubled mind of the pre-reformation, when Satan was a symbol of the conscience. So we get his nightmare of 'Hell' and others of his works. To understand this work of fantasy it is well to remember that this whimsical faculty is that of the dissociation of things that we expect to be associated. This is why fantasy is always a shock. It was the western world that produced the greatest grotesques, with Flanders and Germany at its head. The home of demonology was Asia; its birthplace was Africa and its starkest forms appeared in the work of the north American Indians.

Returning to Fantasy, the finest painter of this art was Brueghel, the Droll of Flanders. He employed fantasy in its purest form. In his picture 'The Land of Cockayne' he shows a delicious wit. It is a finely built picture of three figures; one a soldier, another a student and the third a peasant. They have eaten themselves into insensibility through gluttony. At the back of them is the legendary mountain of porridge through which a newcomer with a spoon in his hand has eaten his way into the land of Cockayne.

The true artist of the land of unreality was Goya who combined reason with fantasy. That he was clear visioned as well is shown in his works 'Caprices' and 'Proverbs.' England also added her example with Rowlandson, the Satirist who laughed at the professions. All these are the forerunners of Surrealism, this perverse movement born of our times which is the chaotic age of Psycho Freudian philosophy of no control. Dali is the acknowledged head of it. He is a Catalonian by birth and is a queer mixture of cruelty and a vivid imagination. When younger he came under the influence of an architect called Gaudi. This man's work is amongst the most curious in the world and can be seen in Barcelona. His architecture has exercised a great power over the works of Dali, which shows in his subconscious imagery. He paints with an incredibly fine talent for the miniature; some of his finest works are no bigger than a post card. This work is really a rebirth of literary and anecdotal painting, and is the exact opposite of Cubism.

Surrealism is the dangerous sister of fantasy as she is the personal nightmare of the artist and could lead to great folly. Dali often superimposes his subjects. He does this to take the mind of the spectator off the storytelling part of the picture and to give an aestheticism to the work. In his 'Persistence of Memory' he has made flexible watches symbolise that time has gone limp, and that the insects on a watch that is on the table have conquered time by sparkling and glittering. His work being so fine in technique (it) has a precious look and so, lacks the strong intellectual feeling of Picasso and the emotional appeal of Berard.

One of the originators of Surrealism was (de) Chirico, who was born in Greece. He has left the group and although he also draws on Freud for his fantasies, his work is different to that of the Surrealists as he is an intellectual dreamer while they are emotional in their visions. In his work there are generally broken columns and mutilated statues that are reminiscent of his childhood. He always gets a feeling of silence and space into his art. His compositions are magnificent in their romantic use of space, far perspective and mellow lights with long shadows, into which, to break their monotony, he sometimes has a child bowling a hoop or a person disappearing into the darkness. His subjects are transposed into restful compositions and although unreal are never horrible, De Chirico is certainly amongst the finest of the Moderns.

Under the category of real fantasy comes the Russian, Chagall, with his Slavonic imagination. His fairy tales that he weaves in paint are as solid as (if) they could come true. There are other painters that do not come under any particular movement (such) as Dufy, the Frenchman, who paints so gaily and wittily. And Modigliani, who had a cubist mind and hereditary Italian instincts, and whose work appeals to the artist as he has such a fine simplicity and never fills his work up with unnecessary 'bits.'

America is not behind with her artists. She has some very fine painters, one of them being (Thomas Hart) Benton U.S.A. born. He was once a strong Cubist and is still abstract in his emotions. There is a fine sense of line in his work and a strong sense of primitive colour but he has a tendency to the pictorial.

So we come to this year of 1938, with the forecast that art must be in an extreme abstractionist manner or it will not fit into the modern architecture. It must create an object of certain lines, balances and relations. This art is suitable for a nation that has found its culture but it is not fit for Australia, who has yet to find her own place in Art, which must be different, as she has forms that no other country in the world has and that have not yet been developed. Her Art will arise when the opportunity comes as America has found hers today.

One of five lectures delivered at the National Art Gallery of New South Wales in 1938, under the auspices of the Carnegie Corporation of New York Educational Service.

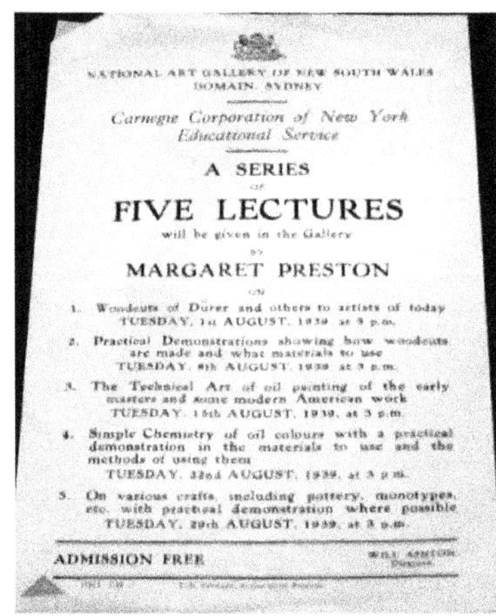

On the Birthday of Jindyworobak

Jindyworobak Review, 1938-1948, Jindyworobak 1948

Jindy is having a 10th birthday. Congratulations Jindy.

First on your surviving until you are ten years old and secondly on the work you have done. You are really a very fortunate magazine as the average life of an infant of your description is about six copies, but it is you and your defunct relatives that spread culture for the nation. These magazines are generally written for and published by young people who have more brains than money. They distribute new ideas, new morals and expend their brains spreading these, generally to a deaf public, but perhaps not so deaf as these works seem to cling to the most unexpected places and so the good work goes on. Now in your case Jindy you have survived although you have chosen the most difficult matter for a public to assimilate, which is Poetry. How many people read poetry? Perhaps not so many as seem indifferent to it. But without it where would England be?

Her greatest claim to culture lies with her poets, Milton, Shakespeare, Shelley, Keats and her living writers of today. So now you see what you are doing, you are giving to Australia an advanced idea that she also with her Australian Poets is developing a culture that will stand by her forever. Your purse is generally empty Jindy but this is an affliction that most small magazines have in common, and alas it is a disease that seems to become aggravated with each edition. But keep bravely working on if you can as without you and your like where could young poets plant their seeds and the world learn of dreams and such things as dreams are made of? Our heartiest congratulations and a sincere wish for a long life and healthy finances.

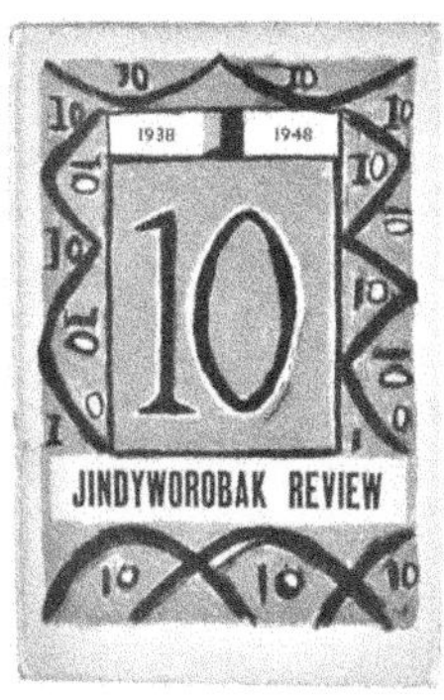

Preston's design for the cover of *Jindywarabak Review 1938-1948* (Jindywarabak Review 1948).

The Orientation of Art in the Post-War Pacific

Society of Australian Artists Book 1942, Ure Smith 1942

The change in the world situation of Australia, made by the War, will compel her artists to readjust their relationship to the Art of the European Continent and Great Britain. They will have to realise that any help they wish culturally lies nearer to their own shores. Australia will find herself at a corner of a triangle; the East, as represented by China, India and Japan, will be at one point, and the other will have the United States of America representing the West. It will be in the choice of one of these corners that the future of Australian Art will lie. Australia is the only country that has had a continuous native Art. Although this factor should help her artists, it is necessary that they should seek from other sources knowledge and inspiration for their craft, thereby combining to produce a National Australian culture. An analysis of the two points of the triangle representing East and West shows vastly different standpoints; the main one for Australia being, which will be the most help without unduly influencing her.

This has been her trouble in the past with European Art. In the Post-War Era she will, it is hoped, be guided but no longer controlled. This will be easier for the artists if they lean to the East, as this Art, especially that of China, has not been raked to pieces to provide new inspirations and aspirations. Chinese Art is so fundamentally correct, that, apart from its aesthetic qualities, it offers continual lessons to the student. The excellence of Chinese landscape is only one example of this perfection. This is the result of the great love the Chinese have for their native soil, and a well-directed training on this subject for many generations. As an instance, they are taught to see the topographical features of the different provinces of the Empire. Every feature of the country is studied and recorded. Students have 'rules', such as the sixteen 'Wrinkles', which are really the geographical formations in a country, or mountains, such as that corresponding to stratification or the cleavage across a stream, or rocks, etc. Everything is minutely recorded and later is reproduced in a spirit of idealism, which is the source and spirit of Chinese painting. This careful training is shown by the difference in the pictures of North and South China. In the North, the landscape is generally magnificent and harsh; especially that near the river Huang He, where the river rushes turbulently through great gorges and chasms. Here the paintings of this part of China have a majestic, rather formal and abstract air. On the contrary, further South, where the river Yangtze, with a few exceptions, runs much more quietly, the paintings have a gentler and more picturesque appearance. A Chinese called Guo Xi has written a wonderful book on this landscape. He gives excellent advice to the student; one remark is, 'not to imitate nature as it is, but to represent it as it appears.' In other words, not to imitate nature as it is, but in its ideal form.

He urges the necessity of objectivity, but at the same time emphasises the importance of subjective expression. This was written about 1020 AD. Fenelossa, a writer of, and a great student of, Chinese Art, says of one painter, Kakei, that 'he was the greatest landscape artist of China, yes, of China and Japan, if not of the whole world'. Landscape is only one form of Chinese Art; their figure work is very fine in line and splendidly composed, and their portraits, of which many can be seen in the Museum in Peking, are effortless in technique and perfect in result. Their sculpture is grand and massive, and so deceivingly simple. So is that of Japan. The wood sculpture in the temples of Nara is astonishing. There is no need to mention the woodcuts of Japan, they are so well known. For the arts and craftsman, and the designer, this country is a Mecca. Kyoto has some good schools of this applied Art; some are State controlled. Japan has produced many fine picture artists in the past, but, strangely, the modern product in plastic Art is mostly horrible - a mixture of bad West and poor East. This is also true of modern Chinese Art. In both instances, fundamentals have been ignored and a base Art has been the result. India also offers her art to the Australian student; all of this wonderland that has been so little explored by the practising artist. Returning to the triangle, with the United States at the other point, the student would find in that country wonderful opportunities for study. There are magnificent museums where the Art of every country in the world can be studied. Fine exhibitions that show work from the Benin Tribes to Picasso, and the National Art of the country is at the disposal of the student to study. North American Art is a matter of great importance, as it has developed into a definite expression of the United States. It is an Art that has perfect technique, as is natural to a country that produces some of the most amazingly accurate mechanism s in the world. Their 'subjects' are mainly material in matter and treatment, which is natural in a country of immense fortunes. The landscapes, which often glow with a definite Italian feeling, have a practical expression about them. The murals of the United States are her great achievement, both in craft and inspiration. Technical ability can be learnt to the last lesson; no device of the old masters, or the new, has been left undiscovered. The teaching of picture-making has been brought to perfection, and the way of living in that country is delightful. In a few words, it can be Post-War Art done in the easy way. The great danger is that of the artist becoming a copyist. This is the danger that Australia is going through now. Originality would be very hard pressed. Studying Art in the West would have none of the trials that would beset the student who turned to the East. There he would find few State museums where Art is collected and laid out for the student. He would have to return to the days of the scholar hunting from temple and town, developing self-reliance and his own thoughts. He would have to hunt for his masters in strange places, and learn from his own intuition how to understand them. No sitting down in Art Galleries or Art Schools, with Art served a la carte, nor any return to Australia with wonderful canvases of great successes. In exchange, he would have found the road that would lead him to an open vision of what his own country is really like. There would be no contamination of a similar civilisation, as, although no student would mind being American 'minded', he would think before becoming an Eastern artist, so he would have to learn to be himself, and Australia would benefit.

Australia stands at the corner ways. Let her remind herself of these facts.

Greek Art leaned heavily on Mongolia, and even went as far as Scandinavia.

Egyptian Art learnt from West Africa.

Europe's Art from snipping bits from all cultures, and American Art from the same sources.

Which end of the triangle will Australian Post-War Artists take?

The Gentle Art of Arranging Flowers

The Home Vol. 5, No.2. June 1924

In the East, the art of flower arranging is a very old one. Legends ascribe the first flower arrangements to those early Buddhist saints who gathered all the flowers strewn by the storm, and, in their infinite solicitude for all living things, placed them in vessels of water.

From such pious beginnings has come to us the gentle art of flower arranging. In a delightful book on this cult by a Japanese artist of the fifteenth century, it says, 'A flower arrangement should be treated like a work of art, made subordinate to the total scheme of decoration.' Sekishun ordained 'that white plum blossom should not be made use of when snow lay in the garden.'

Flowers should be arranged to express something. Thus, when you come into a darkened room on a hot Australian day, and gradually discover for yourself a single lovely white flower in a cool silver vase, how much more restful and beautiful than to find a heaped pot of scarlet geraniums, Iceland poppies, etc.

A flower arrangement should not be moved from the place for which it was designed. How annoying to sit down to a meal with a pot of flowers designed so high that it controls the table; nicer much to have a low bowl full of the colour demanded by your furnishings, and which keeps its place.

Mix your flowers as you do your guests, use due deference to their edges, see how the sharp herringbone fern demands the picotee zinnia as a complement, and roses, with their frail petals, beg the help of the dancing and frivolous Michaelmas daisy. The Japanese flower book says: 'A slender spray of scarlet cherries, in combination with a budding camellia, gives an echo of departing winter, coupled with a prophecy of spring.'

What delights you can give and possess with aesthetic combinations of colour - dark red dahlias, a mass of them, and a few of the primrose yellow and pinky kind, all in a deep blue bowl, and scarlet hibiscus with vivid green and black butterflies resting on their exotic petals. How many arrangements in colour, mass and line could be given, but space does not allow.

Here, then are the last two messages from the flower book: ‘A solo of flowers is interesting, but in a concerto with painting and sculpture, the combination becomes entrancing. Sekishun once placed some water plants in a flat receptacle to suggest the vegetation of lakes and marshes, and on a wall above he hung a painting by Soami of wild duck flying in the air.’ And now the last: ‘That a peony should be bathed by a handsome maiden in a full costume - that a winter plant should be watered by a pale slender monk.’

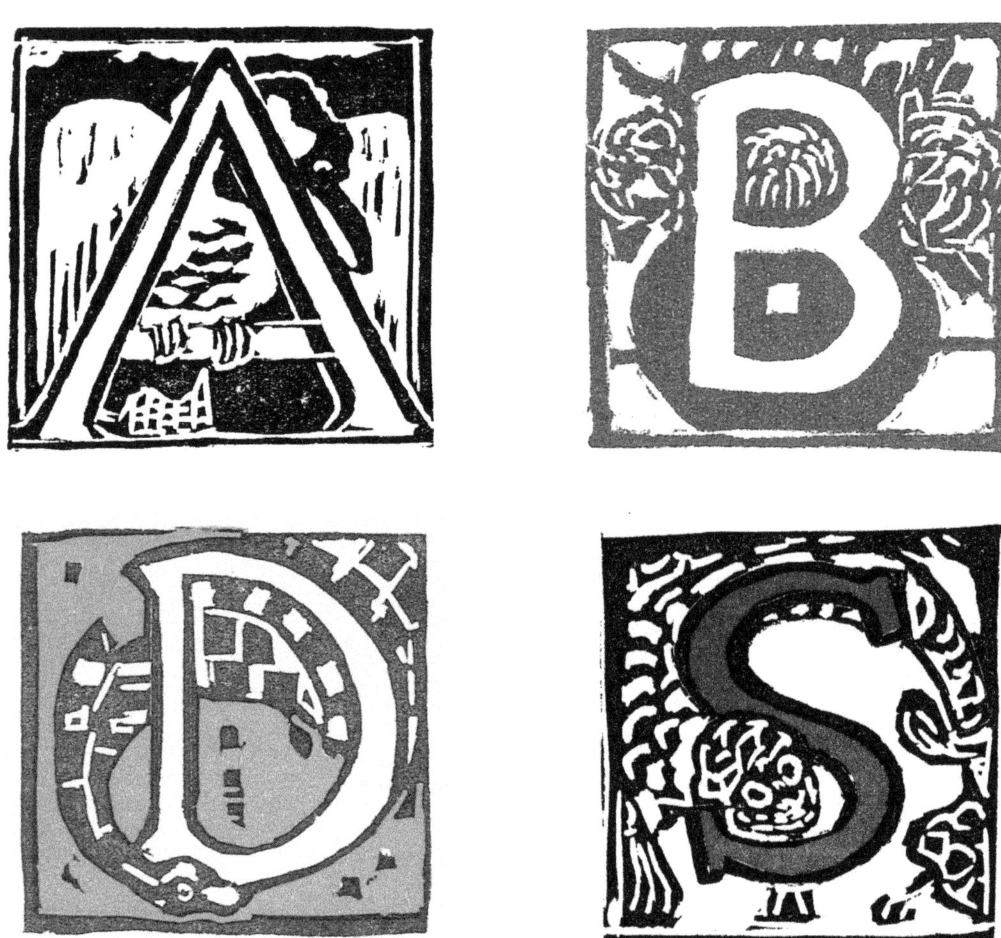

Initials 'A', 'B', 'D' and 'S' (all size unknown) from *Art in Australia,* June and December 1924.

The Best Conditions for Furnishing the Bedroom

Thereby Providing Some Sound Reasons for Not Sleeping Out.

The Home, Vol. 7, No 7 July 1926

Mrs Margaret Preston makes some practical suggestions for arranging a bedroom, keeping in mind that it is the most intimate room in the house.

WALLS

Painted in a pale colour, preferably cream or pink.

WOODWORK

Light in colour, matt in surface work.

CEILING

Plain white, small decorated line separating walls from ceiling.

FLOOR

Seagrass mat, not too big, so that it can be taken up each week.
Outside borders of boards stained or painted.
Grey soft mats for the bedside, etc.

MANTEL

If made of wood, stained a bright colour to match mats and curtains.

ON THE MANTEL

No draperies; a few intimate possessions and a few pet books; coloured linen mats.
Needlework (samples) framed, or a water colour painting - a gaily coloured print would do.
No oil paintings in a bedroom.

CURTAINS

Washing material, something with a bright stripe. Keep rather short.

FURNITURE

Single beds of wood and cane; two or three chairs, one an easy chair with a slip-on cretonne cover, one with a straight back for the dressing table; a low, wide dressing table - all straight lines except the oval mirror. The woodwork to be of a very highly polished nature and the dressing table effects glittering silver or glass.

PICTURES

Water colours or prints.

ORNAMENTS, LAMPS, ETC.

No ornaments. No top lights; they make shadows in the mirror.

THE INDIGENOUS ART OF AUSTRALIA

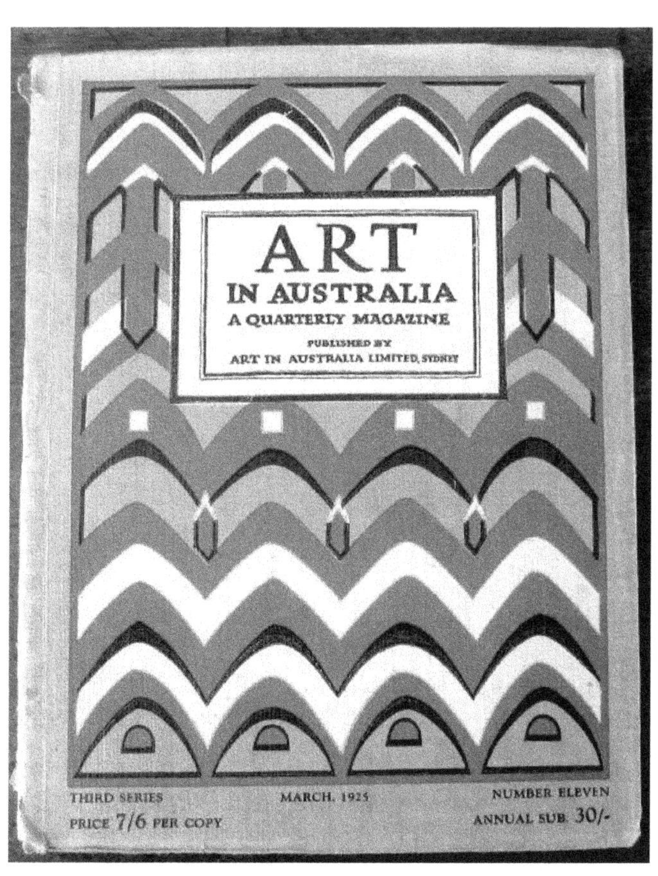

Arts for Crafts

Aboriginal Art Artfully Applied

The Home December 1924

A remark lately made by Mr Hardy Wilson, who has just returned from much travelling to many cities, was that Australians, in their applied art, had not been influenced by the native art which surrounds them. By that he meant that our proximity to Java, China and Japan should have been apparent in our decorative art. I agree with him. In searching around Sydney, for instance, I have only found work copied from these countries or dismal, slightly conventionalised designs of birds, beasts and flowers of our continent such as kookaburras, gum blossoms, etc. Generally there has not been even an attempt made to conventionalise these objects. Downright realism has been used: a large jackass on a square of leather with the cheerful words, 'Greetings from Australia', to represent a cushion cover.

The conclusion seems to be that Australia must honestly confess to having no designs of her own. Taking native flowers, etc., of any country and twiddling them into unique forms will never give a national decorative art.

The need then to try and base our designs on other foundations is obvious. A study of our own aboriginal art may meet with better success. Other countries have not been above profiting by close observation of primitive or foreign races. Many designs for curtains, floorings, etc., are inspired from such sources. Australia could be influenced to its own advantage in the same way.

Look at the design by a very modern Frenchman. It is easy to see by comparison with the Japanese design beside it from where the inspiration is drawn.

The Javanese have influenced western art enormously, both in the textile and theatrical world.

Here is a Kimberley (WA) dancing board that could give you a suggestion for a curtain. I have barely altered the design.

I have a bag made from the ankle bands of a New Guinea savage. The design could have easily been taken from the painted bag in the Sydney Museum.

It may be said that continued abstract designs become wearisome. Look then at the bird on a Buka paddle. There are also fish, etc., for one to draw from. See how they are treated. Do not miss the bark cloth mats. One design represents the track of the hermit-crab and should help dispel the realistic disease. There is nothing more horrible than realism in applied art.

For the potter there are many beautiful forms quite unreminiscent of factories. Beware of that horror - realistic display of fish, fowl or fauna on a pot. The most beautiful pots in the world depend only on their form and colour. Hurry then and use our own material in an Australian spirit before other nations step in and we are left without even having tried for a national spirit in applied art.

The question arises: 'What can Australia do with her native art?' By this is meant the indigenous art of Australia, the Mandated Territory and Fiji - particularly the first two. I had the good fortune to visit the Museum of native art at Rabaul, and was so interested in the collection that was being prepared for the Wembley Exhibition that 1 made many more visits. But this (my good fortune) cannot help the less fortunate designer. So I have gone to the Sydney Museum and studied some of the designs of our aboriginals in order to make a few rudimentary suggestions.

The Australian aboriginal has followed the usual abstract designs that are characteristic of the savage, but I notice that he has used dots much more often than the Fijian or New Guinea native.

There is a dancing board from South Australia that could be very modernly interpreted or applied. I have suggested a cushion cover that could be adapted from the design. It will be noticed that I have tried to keep the primitive feeling, remembering that the savage mind takes no consequence of the beginning or end of his work.

This state of being en rapport with the originator of the design will kill the South Kensington dullness which has pervaded and perverted the decorative impulse of this country. 1 do not mean by this, design without technical knowledge. What 1 mean to convey is - have the knowledge but do not work with exposed knowledge. When one speaks one does not insist on one's knowledge of grammar. Speech is used naturally to convey an idea. Use your art in the same way.

The Indigenous Art of Australia

Art in Australia 3rd Series, No. 11, March 1925

One of the most difficult things there is to do in life is to change one's ideas quickly. The spirit may be very willing, but when one comes to put the new ideas into practical form it seems as if the brain refuses to allow the hand to act; and so one unconsciously reverts to the old ways. In wishing to rid myself of the mannerisms of a country other than my own 1 have gone to the art of a people who had never seen or known anything different from themselves, and were accustomed always to use the same symbols to express themselves. These are the Australian aboriginals, and it is only from the art of such people in any land that a national art can spring. Later comes the individual or individuals who with conscious knowledge (education) use these symbols that are their heritage, and thus a great national art is founded. It is not from book-learning or professional lore which is at the disposal of intellectuals that new life can be drawn. It is on the primitive natural forms that we must depend. In returning to primitive art it should be remembered that it is to be used as a starting point only for a renewal of growth, and a gradual selection must take place to arrive at the culmination. Therefore I feel no loss of dignity in studying and applying myself to the art of the aboriginals of Australia.

Would France be now at the head of all nations in art if her artists and craftsmen had not given her fresh stimulus from time to time by benefiting from the art of her native colonies, and not only her own colonies, but by borrowing freely from the colonies of other countries?

Java has been drained to provide fresh ideas for the craftsmen of the great nations. The indigenous art of Cochin China has given modern sculpture in France a new life. Germany has a national peasant craft, her agrarian policy keeping this always for her. These people have always been the base of German art, but even with such an asset, the art papers of Germany are full of illustrations of the native crafts of Central Africa, showing the need of fresh stimulus and a return to simple symbols. In the beginning was the rough idol crudely carved from wood by the negroes of the Upper Nile centuries ago, and in the end the limpid, smooth, perfect sculpture of the Greeks. So why be scornful of our own heritage?

Let us then commence by having an individual Australian art. Our relation and most intimate connection with our aboriginal art is almost mystic and religious more than merely commercial and industrial. A close study of their forms shows that the gumleaf shape of a sharp triangle and the boomerang are their principal symbols of expression. This they use conjointly with circles. Their totems are decorated with circles and as totemism is one of the origins of art it is ridiculous to deny that the aboriginal of Australia has no definite place in the making of a national art.

Having made my plea for a place in the future art of the world for my country, I will try and show how a beginning could be made. In the study of this primitive work the preconceived ideas generated from schools of art must be placed aside. It will be much easier for the highly intelligent mind to do this than the mind that never thinks for itself but depends on custom and tradition. Starting by accepting the fact that these aboriginal people had emotions that gave them the desire to decorate their shields, etc., it is useful to us to see the rhythm in which many of them are conceived. The cover of this number and one of the illustrations have been taken from a belt belonging to Port Essington, South Australia. The original is in the Sydney Museum. This design has been applied by me in bead work for a handkerchief armlet. It could be used in any colours, and is quite satisfactory in either the small or the large design. Used as a border for a light shade it is easily applied in wool, needlework, stencil, etc. The aboriginal mind has used the boomerang in this design as the motif, and I have brought my conscious knowledge to design with and from it. This feeling of rhythm is very strong throughout these native decorations. The Taphoglyphs (a carved tree indicating a grave) are particularly good and there are many of these in the Museum, one of which is illustrated in this article. I have designed from it for a material that needs an all-over pattern: for instance, people who sleep out of doors need their beds covered, and white coverlets are both ugly and unpractical. Woolpack, hessian, or, if money is easy, burlap with this design worked on it in coarse, bright-coloured wools, or even stencilled, would look well. I did mine with coloured string on woolpack, and found them very practicable as they do not look 'beddy', but smart, and are waterproof and keep out the dust as well.

To aid you in the study of these tree-trunks observe that the boomerang shape has been used with circles. You will not forget that the moon and the sun appear to the aboriginal, as to us, in circular form. These Taphoglyphs are only carvings on the rough bark and so leave the designer a wide field in colour. For the making of rugs the designs on shields are innumerable. The Gulmari shield, West Queensland, could be used by anyone, it is so easy. The mats in my house were black mohair. After very little use they became worn-looking. The backs being made of a kind of canvas I took some chalk and drew on them the few simple lines of the design and filled them in with raffia. The worn side 1 covered with some bright, strong material. The result is that I have two jolly mats that are gay and original. It is to be understood that although the colours should be as simple as possible, those of my design can be altered at will to suit the room in which the article is to be used. As for instance, if your walls are of one colour you are safe to keep your design bright, but if your walls are patterned, then reduce the number of your colours as much as possible to keep the article a quiet mass. There are also many designs suitable for coverings, etc. The Pikan Shield, Russell River, North Queensland, has a butterfly motif. In this design I have barely altered it from the original. It could be applied to decorate furniture. The last-named would make an amusing dado for a child's room, as it represents an unrealistic animal. There is also a bird on a Pikan shield from Russell River, North Queensland, that could yield unlimited designs, and there is a wonderful beetle on another shield showing that the aboriginal designs are not without human interest.

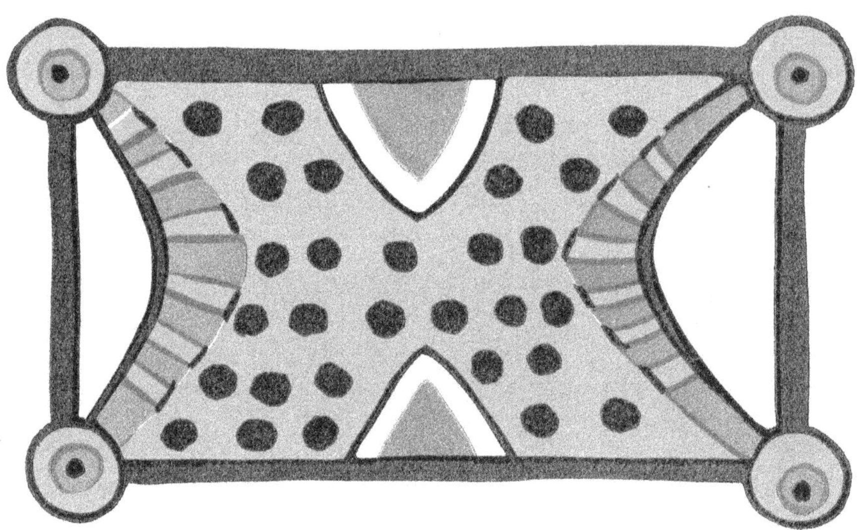

Design from a Golmary shield, North Queensland, which in itself is not adaptable for continuation or repetition. May be applied in mats, cushions or splash mats.

Why not have baskets of our very own? When I returned to Sydney from Europe I thought for the first few days that every woman was off week-ending somewhere, with those curious suit cases they all carry. But 1 found out it was only the national market-bag. In Norfolk Island the women weave, or rather plait, such nice baskets of the local grass. These bags would decorate beautifully either freehand or with a stencilled design. I have a basket in this article showing you the original design. This would not necessarily be the shape; mine is the usual rectangle form suitable for carrying all the small parcels. There are quite a number of painted baskets to be drawn from the museum and the design from the filets or headbands could be made to serve. A Norfolk Island bag could be purchased from any of the Islanders, and it would help them immensely as well. They are now under Australian administration. My bag cost me one shilling. If you do not want to bother sending to Norfolk Island why not have the burlap market-bag decorated with our own designs. I have seen some lovely ones lately in the shops or the arcades, but not one that suggested in any way that it was designed in Australia. Is this fair to our intelligence?

One thing I have not pointed out in these aboriginal designs is their simple colours. As you will see they used only those provided directly by nature: red and yellow ochre and a burnt stick for outlining or blackening masses. And surely when you see the results you will admit that some of them are delightful, restful and simple. No peering shadow pattern to puzzle the mind, no complicated tangle of realistic bunches of flowers, etc., or intricate forms; merely simple decorations, mostly suggested by our own eucalyptus shape, the sharp triangle leaf and its circular shaped flower. These should be the keynote of our national designs. Be as subtle as you like in the use of it, but the using of it in all your designs must have an effect on your work - only, no realism. Can anyone tell me where I can take a stranger in this, my native land to a cafe or playhouse decorated to suggest an Australian atmosphere? 1 have asked again and again but have been told that cafe decoration is virtually unknown. What would Paris be without its decorated cafes. I went to see a new and wonderfully large cinema building the other day. I was impressed with the outside, size, etc., but found the decorations virtually nil, and, such as they were, worse than nil. Surely a place of amusement where one goes to be interested all the time should show some attempt to make not only the stage a draw, but the setting around it. Has anyone attempted to make Australian designs for an Australian play? It would not be Australian to dig up a gum-tree and stick it on the stage. Gum-trees grow better on the Riviera and in California than they do here. Go to the art of our aboriginals to see what is wanted.

Returning to our domestic decorations, as the home is always the reflection of the people who live in it, there is always need for some trifle or the other of a circular shape, and the design of a ceremonial frontlet from South Alligator River, South Australia, could be altered in colour if wanted. It is taken from a frontlet of parrot tails. Border designs are always useful; this one from a dancing board could be drawn and worked by the veriest amateur. For book covers, bookplates, etc., the totem boards are very interesting. They would be useful for this work as they are in line only. One, from Central Australia, I have used in colour to show that, like the Taphoglyphs, the omission of colour does not imply that it is not possible to use colour with them. In two of the designs I have used only one colour. They will be found quite as interesting as the designs with three colours. Almost all of these designs would look well on pottery, as they are all abstract designs. Hand-painted china with our own aboriginal art would surely be valuable.

There is one matter that perhaps is entirely personal. It is that of the colour of the original designs. I have said that the colours should be kept simple. I also think that they should be dense rather than otherwise. I tried some in pale pink and pale yellow and quite lost the native feeling. No doubt someone will arise to make this objection a petty affair, but my feeling about Australia is one of sharp forms and dull colours, notwithstanding the blue skies. Blue is a deep, mysterious colour in opposition to the lightness of pale pink, soft greys, and frail greens.

Do not complain that there is no scope for landscape and figure work in this return to native art. Our landscape teems with forms that are not English or French in shape. If you would see the human figure in a few lines, there is a painted basket from Alligator River, North Queensland, and some very amusing drawings on a filet, North West Australia. Why should not the human figure be treated in this way? The Egyptians simplified it for centuries before their gradual extinction, and these little aboriginal figures have no suggestion of Egyptian or Etruscan art about them. Repetition is merely painting the lily, and this is what we are doing if we insist on trying to adhere to traditional art. When we have started to develop an original art, we will find ourselves discontented with many things about us. We have heaps of objective knowledge in our art, but no spiritual sense, so if you go to the museum and study the art of the aboriginal you are not demeaning yourself or being kind to them. You will find there the simplest and the most elaborate designs which it were well to try and apply in your homes so as to get used to them, and from these small beginnings surely someone will arise who, continually seeing only such simple symbols around him, will apply them in a manner that will make us an individual land in art, as Spanish art is always Spanish, as Italian art is always Italian, etc. Art is not cosmopolitan; it is only the globe-trotter in mind who says that. Our saving grace is our distance from contaminating sources. We have teachers and wonderful prints to help us and the rest must come from ourselves, and the beginning should come from the home and domestic arts. This is the reason that 1 have studied the aboriginals' art and have applied their designs to the simple things of life, hoping that the craftsman will succeed where, until now, the artist has certainly failed.

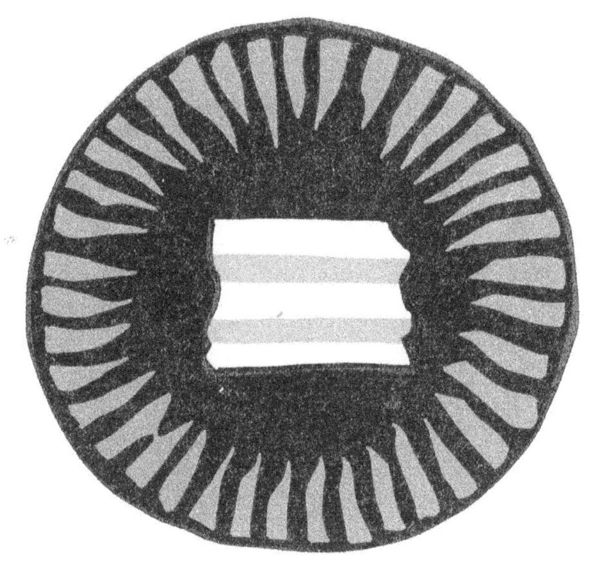

From a ceremonial frontlet, South Alligator River, South Australia. A simple, self-contained design for a cushion.

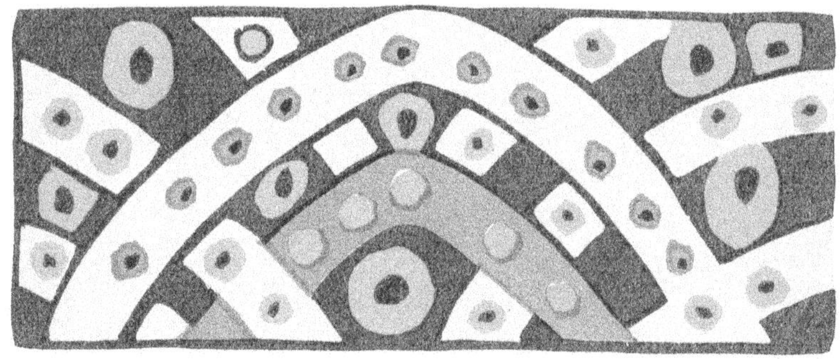

An attractive design from a dancing board, North West Australia. This design is most suitable for continuation as a border for curtains, mats, etc.

What is to be our National Art

Undergrowth, March-April 1927

Art is the tangible symbol of the spirit of a country. No second-class country has produced a national art. What is Australia going to offer to the world as her contribution to the Arts? A magic lantern has given America a place amongst the great nations.

The art of a country is determined by the character of its people.

The national art of England is sport.

The national art of Spain is bull-fighting.

Americans, being essentially a childish people, have originated the cinema. It is their national art.

America has also realised the great fact that there is a limit to the traditional arts, as there is to everything.

Painting, music, architecture, etc., in all countries are the same, differing only in technique, tied to the one man and one landscape. The only opening is in the possibilities of extension.

We Western Europeans have sacrificed to the 'Ancients' the purity and independence of our arts, in that we do not dare to create without one eye on the lofty 'Prototype.'

Art, to fulfil its destiny, requires to be accepted by a nation, or race, and not a few only.

Art in its various manifestations is intensely personal. It is national or racial in itself. There can be no programme to it.

Art never improves, only changes. Its two great properties are infinitiveness and individuality. All the traditional arts from cookery to poetry are universal. They belong to no single nation.

This is an age of science, highly civilised and uncultured. Science also, like the arts, is limited. The cultured man directs his energies outwards. That this is not a cultured but a civilised epoch, is encouraging, as culture keeps tradition in existence. Tradition means trying to live in the style of the olden days. Custom is the guide of the ignorant. Those that object to contemporary art are afraid of their own times.

Science is revolutionary. It gives self-reliance, and self-reliance refuses to light altars to past cycles. What we need is self-development. This is the conscious extension of repertory of experiences. In order to grow there must be youth. National literature begins with fables and end with novels.

Events must move slowly. Those that run at full speed have neither a head nor a heart. Australians have individuality and self-reliance, thus they belong to this age.

What is to be the form of our national Art? Art without form means annihilation. Progress is the illusion of the formless. What magic lantern is to show Australia the way to its national Art?

Acknowledging many sources of wisdom -

When 'Omer smote 'is blooming lyre
He'd 'eard men sing by land and sea,
An' what 'e thought 'e would require
'E went and took the same as me.

The Application of Aboriginal Designs

Art in Australia, 3rd Series. No 31 March 1930

Treating the aboriginal art of Australia in a very simple manner is the only way to arrive at any satisfactory result. To condescend to it from the heights of a school of design education is to make nothing more than unconscious copies of formal studies, with a flicker of naivete culled from seeing and not understanding these primitive efforts. When first I married I could not cook very well, so I bought a cookery book. Without much understanding I started out to make what is considered one of the simplest things, a rice mould. I boiled that rice on and off for three days trying to make it set, then desperately wrote to the author of the cookery book (Sydney Technical College) asking what was the matter with her recipe. Just so. And this is why we have so little venturing into the realm of a new art based on our own natives' efforts. We simply cannot get to the bottom of their minds, it is all just a little too simple for us.

Now let me suggest as a beginning, so that you do not find only blankness in front, that you study No.2 shield (plate 24). Firstly notice that every design by our own aborigines is irregular; this is the essence of their beginnings, for the minds of very primitive beings are not capable of working on set lines. Note that the shield is not evenly divided - that not one of the four upper lines could meet the bottom four, three of them are quite off the mark and yet the result to the eye is not eccentric. Now examine the size of the side masses. Not two are the same, nothing matches.

As an experiment, take the same outside shape - that is, the actual face shape of the shield, and cover it with the same idea but with different shapes, and if your design fails, do not do as I did, write to the originator; just blame your own lack of intelligence. If you manage to get a good design suggested by No. 2 shield, do a dozen or more different abstract shapes from the same shield before starting on No l.

This shield is a good example of lines with the addition of ornament (sharks' teeth) and angles. It also has the intricacy of having a design at the side of the shield different to that of the straight lines of No.2. Note carefully: no halving. Undoubtedly many shields will be brought to light, showing that their art is much more regular than I say, but I have always found when this is the case that outside influence has been at work. Also, please do not bother about what the carver meant in the way of myths, rites, etc.; that is

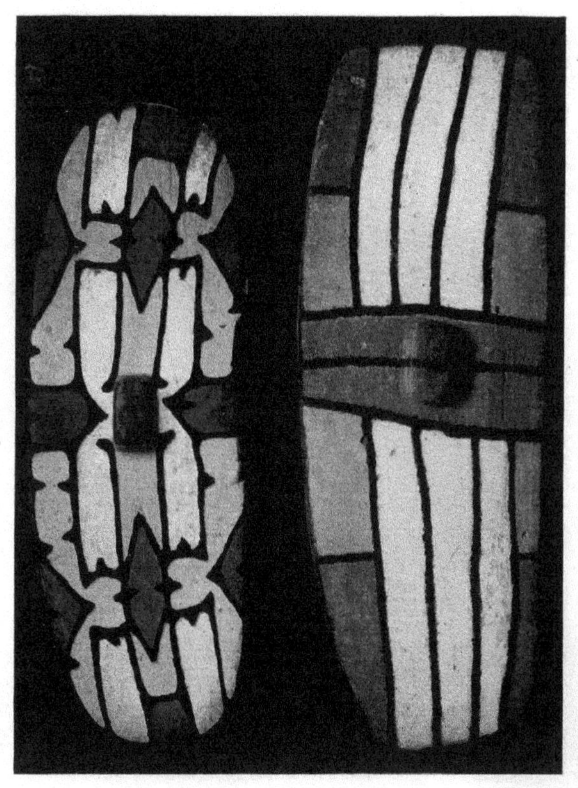

THESE two Boroby or Pikan shields come from Queensland. The shield on the left from the Bloomfield River, Cape York Peninsula, and the right side shield from Herberton in the North-east.

Plate 24.

not the decorator's affair. Now as to the colour, the matter of massing and the primitiveness of the colour is of the utmost importance. The colours at first should be earth colours, such as browns, reds, yellows, white and black. Then if you combine your lines, masses and colours studied from these primitive shields, you probably will be able to produce the same primitive feeling with an educated result. Gauguin achieved this result in his work. If thoroughly studied, it will be found neither erratic nor erotic. It is the Tahitian islander done by a highly educated man.

Tapa does not come from the same type of mind as that of the Australian aboriginal. In the first place, Tapa has to be made, which involves greater mental effort than merely picking up a piece of wood: so that although the maker of Tapa is a primitive, he is a developed primitive and in advance of our own aborigines.

When working on a piece of Tapa it is not advisable to try to condense the whole piece. Take half only and once more dissect. Remember their designs are not to rote and rule, so that any part of them serves for the purpose of dissecting.

I have chosen as simple pieces as possible. It is better for a study such as that of primitive art to try to get near to the genesis of mind as well as of matter. As to the application of the designs, keep them for the impersonal things at first, such as tray cloths, door stops, crockery, etc., but not for, say, golf or sport stockings. I have seen these garments with the exact fish design from an Essington (South Australia) belt. The result was fearsome; this, as in the rice mould episode, was misunderstood energy.

You may think that severe lines without effects front objects (as animals, etc.) dull, and will lead to weariness. I think not. Abstract designs are absolutely essential for such material as pottery and glass. The Greeks were certainly on the down grade when they started to plaster their exquisitely formed vessels with figures, the sense of form being interfered with. Besides, the pots became pictures, and this is not what pots are meant for.

So please do not forget: no realistic designs on very utilitarian objects. Be aboriginal.

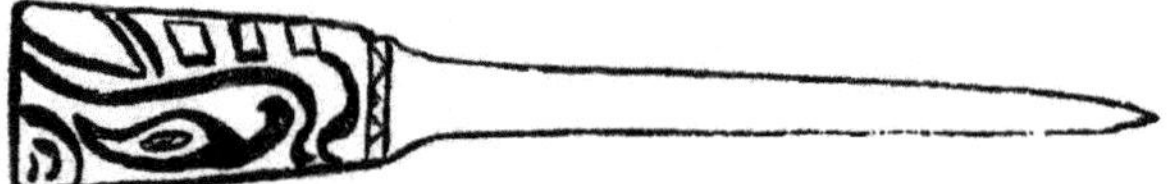

Design applied for paper knife
in bone, wood or metal.

Away with Poker-Worked Kookaburras and Gumleaves

Sunday Pictorial, April 6th 1930

Australian aboriginal art has always been considered a negligible quality and quantity, and a slogan has travelled the world 'as low in intellect as an Australian aborigine.'

On this principle, no artist has even bothered to explore the possibilities of using aboriginal designs, and applying them to furniture, rugs, china, wallpaper, textiles, and other things used in everyday Australian life.

The work of the natives is so primitive in design and colour that the art of no other country can offer such a simple base for the student. Most intricate designs can be built up, and it is high time we started to make our homes more Australian in atmosphere. In articles manufactured here there has been an attempt to make them characteristic.

Even if borrowing from aboriginal designs means the production of a tripper or souvenir art, it is better that this should be so as a commencement than that Australian motifs should be applied in a bastard way.

Oh, those wretched kookaburras, gum leaves, and wattle blossoms done on cushions in a Kensington (England) school-of-design manner! One aboriginal prayer let there be - may no one ever give me a suede cushion cover worked with a kookaburra, or horrors of misapplied energy in the form of paper-cutters, vases, and ash trays of indiscriminate designs, such as one sees in nearly every shop in Sydney!

'High-brow' art is not desired, but impudent art is not necessary - impudent in the sense that these stamped- worked gum leaves and kookaburras are degrading the art sense of a young nation.

The time has come for us to establish an Australian school of design. In the Australian Museum there are hundreds of native relics which the student may examine; the authorities always being most courteous and helpful.

The natives have felt the harshness of their conditions and only constructive forms interested them. Their ideas are those of a new race of people struggling for expression, unlike the Maori art, which belonged to a race which has progressed as far as it can.

The art of Spain is brutal; British art, charming and suave; but Australian art, as revealed by the natives is austere, like our scenery. What could be more austere than the Blue Mountains.

The student must be careful not to bother about what myths the carver may have tried to illustrate. Mythology and religious symbolism do not matter to the artist, only to the anthropologist.

In building up new designs from those supplied by the blacks, let the student keep to the harsh, crude facts, and scorn sentimentality, colour does not matter, only form. But this will be difficult for young modernists to carry out, so many of them depending too much on the addition of colour to their work and not enough on the simplicity of form.

Then, too, these scholarships which send young Australian abroad to study mean that subconsciously the students develop a European outlook. Let us have no travelling for our budding artists!

There are quite capable teachers here, and the students will learn to see Australia with the mental eyes of an Australian, instead of being contaminated by the influence of Continental schools.

‘Forms that will suggest Australia’

Excerpt from the article, Some Recent Paintings.
Art in Australia, 3rd Series, No 59. May 1935

I am trying to find even one form that will suggest Australia in some way. 1 am trying to simplify my colour to my form - to work as simply as to all appearances my country is. Australia is a country that gives the impression of size and neutral colour. To give this impression on canvas or woodblocks 1 find it necessary to eliminate ‘dancing’ colour and to heap my light and shadows. 1 have abandoned the regulation yellow-colour sunlight and made form explain light, because 1 feel that Australia is not a golden-glow country but a country of harsh, cool light. In my effort to give a feeling of sharp flatness I force my compositions with as much solid light as possible. I am trying to suggest size, and to do this I am eliminating distracting detail.

My subject as subject I ignore. My fondness for painting banksias is due only to the simplicity of their form and colour. They allow the other material in the composition to have an equally dominant position in the scheme without appearing to do so. I want stark realism without imagery: the elements of my compositions are not literary symbols. In my search for forms which will suggest Australia 1 prefer woodblocking to painting, for the wood hinders facility and compels the worker to keep forms in his compositions severe.

Paintings in Arnhem Land

Art in Australia, 3rd Series No. 81, November 1940

It has been for a long time the accepted idea of the world in general that the Australian aboriginal is in the lowest grade of humanity. This unfortunate impression should be completely altered after a study of his pictorial and decorative art.

The art of the Australian aboriginal must not be confused with that of the Polynesian or European. Polynesian art is repetitive. It is restricted in form, and it is concerned principally with the 'pageant' aspect in art. Modern European art has gone either Victorian or Freudian with a story attached to it.

The work of the Australian aboriginal has no 'display' about it. There is no curious desire to astound, as in the Maori 'tongue' art, nor imitation of 'gods', as in New Guinea and native art generally. It is never repetitive. The geometrical designs are balanced, but they are never duplicated. Their caves, rocks, and bark, and they themselves, are painted, either for totemic purposes or for ornament, with strong outlines and clean, unmuddled colour. This art can stand comparison with the early primitives of Italy. The Italian artist prepared the material for his design with a ground of one colour, and drew the design carefully in this one colour. The Australian aboriginal, having a mind different from a civilized Italian, either prepares his material with one colour or works straight onto the self-coloured bark or rock. He does not draw his design with his colour, but onto it.

Simplicity in the use of colour is another point of comparison. The Italian primitive never used more than three colours. All gradations and changes in colour were made by glazes. The Australian aboriginal, being more primitive, uses earth colours only - red and yellow (ochre), white (gypsum), and black (charcoal). As he is an earth spirit, he reasons that there is no green or blue earth, so why use other than earth colours? If in some aboriginal decorations blue is used, these tribes have come into contact either with Malays (indigo) or with civilization (the blue bag).

The Italian primitive never mixed his colours. Neither does the Australian aboriginal artist. He uses pure colours only, and depends on form and on his sense of decoration. No shadows nor vivid lights, but simple flat colour laid in fine juxtaposition.

There are other comparisons that can be made, but as each of these primitives has his own especial characteristics, one or two of these that mark aboriginal work will be pointed out. Firstly, it must be understood that the various tribes have different subjects. Those of Central Australia are exceptional with their geometrical designs. The fish and plant designs of the Northern Territory and of Arnhem Land are unique, and the symbolic paintings in caves in the northern Kimberleys are thoughtful and artistic. Their combination of subjective mind with realistic eye has produced work that is original. In some of the hunting scenes the relative size of man to animals will often appear out of proportion. But the aboriginal regards his subject as being of the first importance, and in the hunting scenes the animal stands for food, which is the 'subject' in his mind. The fruit pieces will often have this same 'objectiveness'. A yam will be drawn as a very large fruit, and attached to its sides will be small forms that represent leaves and flowers.

The great difficulty for serious students of aboriginal art lies in the remote situation of most of the paintings. This can be overcome to a certain extent by visiting the museums, which generally have a fine collection of shields and other articles. There are also excellent publications that can be used as text books, such as Australian Aboriginal Art by F.D. McCarthy, of the Australian Museum in Sydney.

The illustrations to my article are situated in a rock shelter in Arnhem Land, near Oenpelli, on the East Alligator River, about two hundred miles from Darwin. To reach the site, we travelled in a Puss Moth plane, which flew for two and a half hours over various rivers and herds of water buffalo. This was quick time, as a lugger would have taken five days, and even then we should have been some distance from Oenpelli. The rock shelter is three or four miles from Oenpelli, and the paintings are on the top of a high hill, on the ceiling of an overhanging rock. This part of the journey can be done either on foot or in a motor lorry. As the journey is across rough, trackless country, it is necessary to have aborigines as guides. Incidentally, the heat is terrific.

There are a few drawings on the high cliffs that surround the rock, but the main work is on the rock ceiling. Unfortunately, another rock painting is quite obliterated, as the aborigines have used these cliffs as shelter in the wet season, and smoke from their fires has blackened one ceiling completely. It is considered by the local Myall (Aboriginal) that these paintings were done long years ago by hunters caught in the wet season. The rock shelter is in excellent condition, and has never been used for fire-making. The paintings are in the usual red ochre, black, and white, which have been mixed with fat, such as that of the goanna. The little dug-out cups in which the colours were mixed are still in good condition on the rock floor. The rock ceiling has its natural ochre ground, on which the fishes are outlined in black, white, or red. Time and light have faded some of the red, so that many of the fish have acquired a pinky colour. Away from the light, the colours were stronger, so that the whole effect was of a charmingly graded mural.

The work is that of the Kakadu tribe, and, with a few exceptions, it depicts fish of all kinds. The species of fish is easily discernible by its size and shape. The shapes are mostly drawn so as to show the backbone, the dorsal arches, the intestines, and the edible part of the fish. Many are superimposed with parts of other fish, snakes, and odds and ends. There are also finely drawn turtles, snakes, and fancy creatures belonging to the fish totem. The whole ceiling of the rock, which is about 30 feet long, is covered with paintings. It is full of colour and interest, both from an artistic and from a scientific point of view.

Outside the cave are walls of high rock, some decorated by long, attenuated figures of spirit men; others by drawings of kangaroos, and yet another with a curious drawing of a gnome. The surrounding district contains many other paintings, but it is difficult country to travel over, and demands the constant service of the aborigines as guides. As it is not possible for the average artist to travel to these places, he must depend on the museums. Work studied there should be used with the technical knowledge of the trained artist. If this is done, there is a chance for Australia to have a national art - an art taken from its primitive peoples, the Australian aborigines; an art for Australia from Australians.

New Development in Australian Art

Australia National Journal, May 1st 1941

To the artist one practical result is worth a library of book-lore. The motto of today should be, if you can't paint, write about it. So the artist is pestered with every kind of art critic. This has only led him further and further into the crime of making a poor, weak, imitative art. Australia has not escaped this curse. She has ignored a fine simple art that exists at her own back door. It was to learn what this art could do to help clean up the minds of our people and give them a national culture that 1 have given many years of my life to the study of this aboriginal art.

My travels from The Coorong, South Australia, to Ravensthorpe, West Australia, to the Hawkesbury, New South Wales, to Arnhem Land, Northern Territory, and around and about the continent, makes a pilgrimage worthy of the hunting of the Snark. At last I feel I have cornered a little bit of him - the 'him' being aboriginal art.

My conclusions are that this work can be so helpful that I am now trying to apply it to my European education. My travels have taught me that the aboriginal artist was a one-way minded person. He knew his subject, so that there was no need to bring home dead whales, wallabies, or pieces of landscape. These objects were not only familiar to him through his factual eye, but with his mind's eye as well. Every characteristic, obvious and hidden, was known to him. Knowing these things, he would put his knowledge on to the rock without break or shadow. He used his colours with system and simplicity, so few yet so sufficient that they gave dignity to the simplest subject.

His symbolism he carried throughout his work, which is spontaneous and often intricate.

These facts 1 found for myself; now I am trying to apply them. Knowing the New South Wales ranges well, 1 have tried to paint them with stark truth, copying the natives in eliminating the western idea of time and place. 1 am trying to show by form that it is not necessary to rely on colour to suggest any object. 1 know that art is of the mind and a picture a replica of the mind's vision. A camera-mind producers a camera picture, and this type of mentality has never belonged to the aboriginal.

So I am humbly trying to follow them in an attempt to know the truth and paint it, and so help to make a national art for Australia.

Australia is the only country in the world that has rock cave painting consistently present. It is the only country in which rock painting still flourishes as the normal expression of its aborigines.

Australian aboriginal art is symbolical and hyper-realistic.

It must not be judged from its technical quality, but from its introspective character.

The drawings and rock carvings are a truthful art. They are realism in a wider sense than that recognised by European Art.

Aboriginal Art represents not the object alone from which it is drawn, but with the essential truths which may or may not be visible to the human eye.

The study of the work of the Australian aborigines is nearly exhaustless.

It is symbolism. Through its Totemism (inherent vision) it opens up a new world for the Australian artist.

Know your subject and paint your knowledge.

Aboriginal Art of Australia

Catalogue of Carnegie Exhibition 1941

Australian aboriginal art has for a long time been under a cloud as belonging to a people on the lowest level of civilisation. But the aborigine is an artist - a true and sensitive artist whose work should be studied and treated with the respect that is due to true art.

The aborigine, it is true, has a different standpoint to the artist of our western civilisation. On comparison, however, the advantage often lies with the aborigine.

Australia is the only country in the world today that has rock cave painting flourishing as a normal expression of its people. I do not refer to rock carving, as that does not appear to be practised any longer.

The aborigines' work can be divided into three types: (1) hyper-realistic, (2) symbolistic, (3) naturalistic.

His realism has a wider ideal than European art. A fish will be painted with both its outside form and inside essential organs. With fruit it is the same. The outer form, the seeds and so on.

These people paint and draw with knowledge from the mind more than with mere visual perception.

With their symbolistic work, they depend on line and form only. A circle may suggest a fly and the lines radiating from it the swarming of flies. A set of wavy lines may mean rippling water and the lines circling about them the wind causing the disturbance.

With their naturalistic work they aim at giving the whole form in one outline without any concession to detail. They do this both in their line and colour work. They never aim at perfection, but at a semblance of it. Their art is spontaneous. Their colour sense is in no way different to that of all primitive races. It is restricted in range, but as they come in contact with civilisation it increases.

As a general rule earth pigments are used, yellow and red ochres - gypsum or wood ash for white and charcoal for black.

They always had a knowledge of vegetable dyes. This is apparent from their use of blue made from a berry growing profusely in the Olary district of South Australia, and the scarlet used in the work in the Kimberley region which is extracted from a plant growing there. Their brushes are twigs chewed to make them pliable and then tied together with hair. For fine spots they fill their mouths with liquid pigment and squirt it on the work.

There are three ways in which an aborigine paints - by stencil, freehand and impression. The third is done by putting the hand into liquid clay and slapping it on to the wall.

For rock painting, the pigment is ground in rock holes or shells and is mixed with a substance such as goanna fat to make the mixture stick on the rock. This work is done by the freehand method. A strong outline in a dark colour is drawn and then filled in with colour. The pattern and colour is not a chance affair, but a deliberate design.

Central Australia holds pride of place for carved drawings on wood and stone, and New South Wales is full of rock drawings. The Melville and Bathurst Islands specialise in beautifully designed and painted grave posts.

The most interesting work from a painter's point of view is probably the bark paintings of Arnhem Land.

The rock carvings of New South Wales are extremely naturalistic and are done in firm outline only.

The art of the aborigine has for too long been neglected. The attention of Australian people must be drawn to the fact that it is great art and the foundation of a national culture for this country

An Art in the Beginning

Society of Artists Book 1945-1946, Ure Smith 1946

Australia should become a land of artists. It is our heritage from our aboriginal painters, who, it is said, worked at their art some two thousand years ago (Mutawintji), and who continue to work to this day.

This country has produced a western art from about 1826. It is reminiscent, and to this date differs very little in its basic principles. The subjects and techniques have changed according to their times, but the antipodean feeling has remained. This is why a study of the ideas in our aboriginal art has been made and an attempt to apply their elements with that of western training.

Only the cave, bark, and rock paintings are studied in this article. The decorative designs on weapons, utensils, and on everything that interested these people, even to decorating their bodies, is a study in itself. The totemic part of their work is another branch of study which does not come into the latitude of plastic art, any more than the religious views of the Van Eycks in their magnificent, aesthetic and cultural art. It has been said and written that if an aboriginal art of a country is taken as a direction, it leads to either a dead end or a side track. That is quite true if the artist uses it to produce pseudo work, but if it is used as something from which the essentials of nature and the spirit of the country can be learnt better than from the intellectual achievements of periods of great culture, then it is possible that a beginning can be made for an art for this country that will not be a replica. As Herbert Read says, 'The virtue of a plant is in its seed, its form is implanted in it from its first shoot'.

Every race has its own culture, and it seems as if they all start from a common cult of imposing certain colours and forms to emphasise their real character. This our aboriginal art does. Their artists have the skill to use solid shapes to show their ideas, they look at nature to get form and the external order of it, to see the inner life of things, because they have no traditional or academic inhibitions.

All aboriginal art has an idea behind it. The aboriginal artist works with a distinct reason, either totemic or aesthetic. Quite different from that of 'child' art, which is that of something seen, remembered or imagined. For the student to work from this native art it is necessary that he should try to follow the working of the artist's mental attitude. Take, for instance the pictures he has made of animal tracks, and especially of night hunting beasts; in these he has retained the mental pictures of the tracks rather than that of the animal he did not see. Then, again, in his superimposing and the use of the inner forms of his objects, such as fish and fruit. He remembers the combination of his objects and the food he eats, so he scratches or paints his ideas in this fashion. He uses the simple earth colours, because he has not been trained to see other than earth colours; he is an earth spirit, but goes beyond the early people, who see only black and white.

There is no knowledge of perspective; he does not need it. For a practical illustration, look at a native kangaroo hunt. The artist thinks this is to be a picture of a kangaroo hunt. So he makes the kangaroo his principal interest; next the spear, and then himself, who is less important. A trap can catch an animal, but there must first be an animal. Perspective is only a device to explain; his work needs no explanation; his masses tell their own story.

My application of this art is shown in 'Flying Over the Shoalhaven River'. I have thought, 1 am flying over the river; the earth was an addition. I concentrated on my clouds, remembering the laws of colour and form; the river is the same, and lastly the earth. In my flower pieces it is the form that I wish to emphasise, and I use only the simplest of earth colours, so that the mind will see before the eye. My 'Dry River' is another example showing the form that is peculiar to this country. I know that the work is objective and has no emotional value, but what is the use of emotion if the artist does not know that art has certain definite rules and how to obey them?

The construction of a national art can't be 'made', because it must come from the subconscious and express the national characteristics and temperament; but the growth of such an art must be slow and begun from the conscious before the subconscious. This aboriginal art, that seems easy, is not so in its essence; it should be used as a starting point. The artist must do his own work, and the study of our native art used to clear the mind of European standards, but not of training, which is part of our civilization.

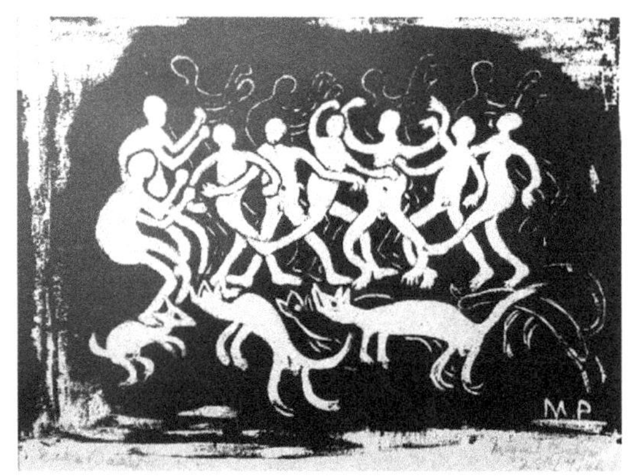

'Native Ballet', screenprint, 1946, 27 x 34 cm, from *Society of Artists Book 1946-47* (Ure Smith, 1947).

My Monotypes

Margaret Preston's Monotypes, Ure Smith 1949

William Blake, one of the world's greatest artists, made some of his finest painting with the aid of this Monotype medium. He, it is said, wanted to get a different technique for his watercolours, so he found a way of using Monotype as a ground for his work. He never disclosed how he did it. The method died with him.

As an artist William Blake stands alone, because in his work, and particularly in compositions such as the 'Waiting Virgins', he has shown the human figure as something sublime. The fierce subconsciousness of another world permeates all his art. The human form becomes superhuman surrounded by visions. He died in 1827, seeing Heaven as he went. The Melbourne Art Gallery has a collection of his drawings.

Though the Monotypes in this book were inspired by him, they do not presume to have any relation to his work; it is the principle in the method that is the connection. No apologies are offered for them; they have been made by a simple technique; they are Monotypes and are offered as such.

Since I am an Australian by birth and an artist by profession it is only reasonable that the subjects of the pictures in this book should be Australian, as one should understand one's people and country best. On that premise and a general study of Australian Aboriginal Art these works were made.

General Smuts once said: 'The temper of South Africa is curious and full of individuality; they are only a handful of whites, and each private thinks himself a general'. This speech also represents Australians. We think and act as if we are the freest people in the world; but are we? Certainly not in our cultural side. Our pictorial art is tied to tradition or in copying the various movements in painting and sculpture in the Antipodes. Now and again the spirit that is Australia has cropped up, in odd pieces of literature and in the rhymes of our minstrel poets who sang with a carefree jingle of outdoor life and of the people. We are a nation of people who are growing up and who should not acquire a counterfeit culture by borrowing the intellect of all countries. This is not written in defence or in an appeal for a national art; it is written with the idea that some of these Monotypes may show the potentialities of an art that has intellectual differences from that of other countries.

That an indigenous art can help or affect a civilized taste has always been denied; this denial is true in part, as this type of work never expresses the purely spiritual as do Blake and Rembrandt. There is much to learn from it, and as no one can teach the Infinite, a few words about this type of work may not be unwelcome.

Australia has the good fortune to have a native race who paint and draw as they have always done, and with a few exceptions look on their work as essential, more than merely covering a rock, bark or ground with forms. They feel dimly something they contact in it that they, like ourselves, vaguely understand. Their culture is of the clan; in some parts of the continent the artists of the tribe drew on granite rocks, and never painted; this at Yunta, South Australia. In Arnhem Land they paint on rock faces and ceilings and draw with colour; other parts have tribes that produce decorative work, and so on.

It is not suggested that their work should be used as a 'model' for the educated painter, but an aesthetic form that is of our land, which can offer the smallest help, should be gratefully taken and a few words of appreciation not come amiss.

Their work can be divided into three types - Hyper-realistic, Symbolic and Naturalistic. This art is never an attempt at rigid realism, they represent but never duplicate; this last feature is hardly possible, as all their designs are from memory or imagination. The work has no particular technique, and uses symbolic perspective and never scientific; their designs are nearly always asymmetrical. Although the fewest colours are used, the work does not look dull or overcrowded. Their realism takes a wider scope than that of European work. A fish, animal, or man is painted with both the internal structure and outside form; they draw what they know as well as what they see. As an example of their symbolic work, a circle is used to indicate flies, and lines radiating from it a swarm of flies. A set of lines may mean rippling water, and lines running around them, wind causing the disturbance.

In their rock paintings they are true fresco painters, painting with earth colours directly on the absorbent surface of the wall. They know how to superimpose without muddling. In their huge anthropomorphic figures they realise that size can be symbolic. Theirs is abstract vision that is without human feeling but that of fear, as in their Kimberley Wandjina paintings, which have heads without mouths but have eyes and a nose. No imagery is attempted with the human form. Their Bora, or sacred ground drawings, should be seen if only through the medium of photographs. The designs are made on the ground of piled or painted earth; they are large in extent and big in design. The name Bora is derived from Boora, the belt of manhood which is conferred on the young men in a ceremony on entering adult life. These designs are destroyed after the rite. A distinctive thing about their work is that they do not 'group' their objects; their pictures are generally of separate things not connected with the whole subject.

These Monotypes are only a few of their forms to be found in their art. The Bimbowrie landscape in this book is from an example of their work in conjunction with that of the trained artist. In this picture there is a complete disregard for scientific perspective. The cave where this work was found was in an almost inaccessible spot, in the heart of an immense sheep station in South Australia.

The fish picture is another version of their art; the flat colour of the background with the lined design on it and the fish in pattern with the outsides and insides of equal value. There are no shadows, as these are never used in aboriginal art. It must be understood that this work has not been copied from the originals, but the principles applied. Fish are the most often used as guides for representation on the rock paintings of Oenpelli, on the border of Arnhem Land in the Northern Territory. This place is an artist's paradise for seeing this kind of work, as on the eastern side of Oenpelli rise hills and in their rock hollows all kinds of paintings are to be found. The Kimberleys, in the North-Western District of Australia, has curious work, known as the Wandjina. They are different in sizes and are unlike any other of our aboriginal art.

Returning to the pictures in this book: there is one of a still-life with some eggs; notice could be taken of the snakes half surrounding the composition. There were two reasons for the use of these forms; one to try to give another effect to a still-life apart from grouping and technical excellence, and to produce a different aesthetic quality - in this work that of being slightly sinister. The other reason was to create a still-life that would owe its existence to this country, and not to Holland or another nationality. The basin of eggs was necessary to give a firm line for the eye to rest on. Superimposing part of the black egg over the white gives interest, and is purely aboriginal.

On another page will be found a picture of a billabong; this is a backwater to a river. Two or three colours were used in the design for this work; they are quiet in tone, as the billabongs of Australian waters are sombre. There seems always to be a miasma about them, perhaps rising from the heavy air of the enclosed shallow water and rotting wood as well as the circling of insects and flies. The quietness and simmering look was its attraction. The technique in painting the billabong was changed from that of the fish and Bimbowrie pictures, as it had an expression of 'feeling', a representation of which the native artist never attempts.

The Monotype 'Drought Mirage' was made from the memory of a trip in the back country when it was drought-stricken. The parched land bred mirages of phantom trees in gay blue water, trees were reflected in it, the earth was yellow and gaunt, thirst-stricken kangaroos weakly jumped by. Trees without foliage were blackened by continual heat and dead kangaroos lay around. Black stones littered the land, only the mirage was gay. The animals did not see it; they passed, never raising their heads. Accordingly, the treatment in this picture had to be as simple as possible, depending on outline and flat colour. No attempt could have been made to reproduce a lifelike animal; the only gay spot was the mirage. In this work the only leaning on aboriginal art is in the perspective. The passing kangaroos and mirage were the interest, although, according to scientific perspective, the two dead animals in front should have been twice as large as they have been represented. There are two perspectives, one for the artist and the other for the architect.

In the 'Bush Track' an attempt has been made to give the rough and tumble of trees without design or any other purpose than that of covering space, as the native artists have done in their well-covered rock decorations. The rocks in the front are foreign forms introduced in the same way as Totem forms are often added to a wall covered with hands.

In 'Pacific Ocean' an essay has been made to give an upright perspective instead of a receding one; the underlying blue colour that seems to be part of the Australian bush has been used for this. The two stark trees with the patterned Banksia trunk hold the hills with their amorphous foliage in place. This is a landscape of a well-known place. The scene was memorised and applied; it is realistic, but not a copy.

The decoration 'Bananas' is a study in earth colours and in the asymmetrical balance of aboriginal art, a decoration that fills space without accepted rules. This aspect of native art is accepted as the most useful. Its application can cover so many useless or useful articles.

Discussing the flower paintings is another matter. Few flowers have been depicted by the aborigines; when they have been done, the work shows not only the flower but the whole plant; the roots are of equal importance as the blossoms, even more so, as they are made into strong designs. There is no attempt at making a resemblance. The main outline of the flower is represented with lines around and in the shape. That they are rarely used in their art is in accordance with native life in Australia, which at its best has always been hard. Flowers, not being edible nor necessary to placate, would not be thought worthwhile reproducing. Probably these early tribes did not see them as flowers. It has been proved that primitive people are not gifted with a wide colour sense, and blossoms would not mean anything more to them than any other foliage. The flower studies shown are all of Australian flora.

In the 'Native Flower' group the flowers are the creation of a twentieth century artist, while the bowl and background belong to a primitive aboriginal art; it is by no means that of a children's craft. It is made from observation, an inherent sense of design, and in their Decorative, Totemic and Symbolic drawings they show a definite sense of 'plan', whereas children's art is generally imitative of something seen or being seen. It is as realistic as they can make it with their limited knowledge, and can always be labelled.

Children depend largely on bright colours, which are splashed about with a happy ignorance. Their outline sense seems to be lacking. To compare their work with that of the designs of the Bora ceremonies and other work, such as that in Oenpelli, is not reasonable.

As it has been pointed out, this native work is not meant to be in any way a substitute or foundation or anything else but a help to a student artist who wishes to explore for himself the possibilities of his craft. For such a student a few words of help can be given. Naturally it is better to see the actual work of these people in its surroundings and the paintings where they are, but owing to so many difficulties in the way of travelling to see even the work of one tribe it is better to use the Museums and Art Galleries. In these buildings every kind of aboriginal art can be studied, from decorated dilly bags to painted skulls. Each museum has different collections from various anthropological and other explorations in Australia, but even these galleries have not sufficient reproductions of aboriginal rock paintings and engraving sites.

There is also another point in studying in the museums; they have as well as Australoid art the different cultures of the Melanesian and Polynesian, of which it is necessary for the student to have some knowledge to compare with his own.

This book of Monotypes is not meant as a guide or in praise of a primitive art, but as an acknowledgment for help that has been acquired from it, which could not have been appreciated if there had not been a thorough educated foundation. Every artist must work from his own temperament. It has been said, 'The part that cannot be explained is the only part that matters,' and so it seems as if the student must fight out his own problems.

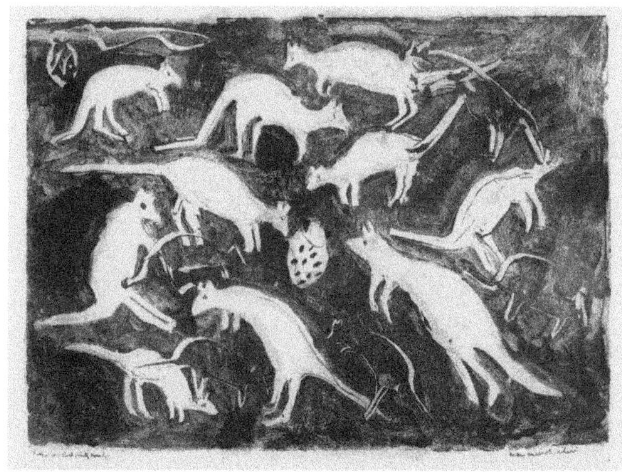

'Kangaroos', monotype, 1946, 30.2 x 40.6 cm, from Preston's *Monotypes* (Ure Smith, 1949).

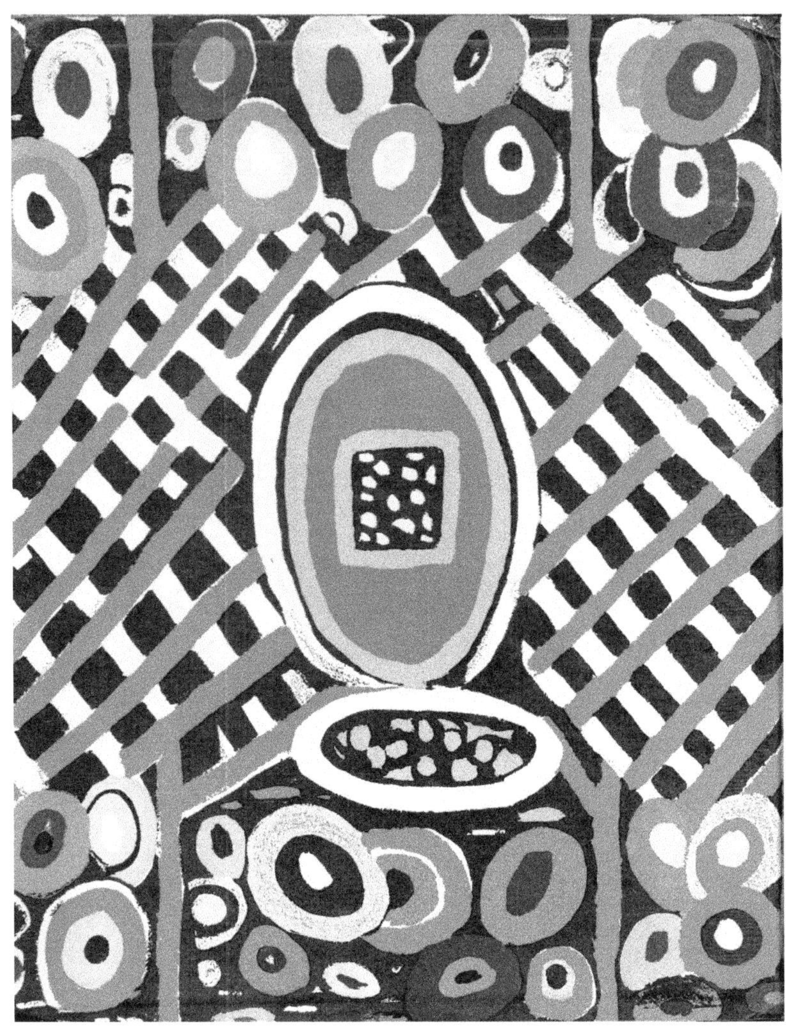

(Aboriginal Design), colour monotype, size unknown, endpapers for *Monotypes* (Ure Smith, 1949).

ARTISTS'

GROUNDWORK

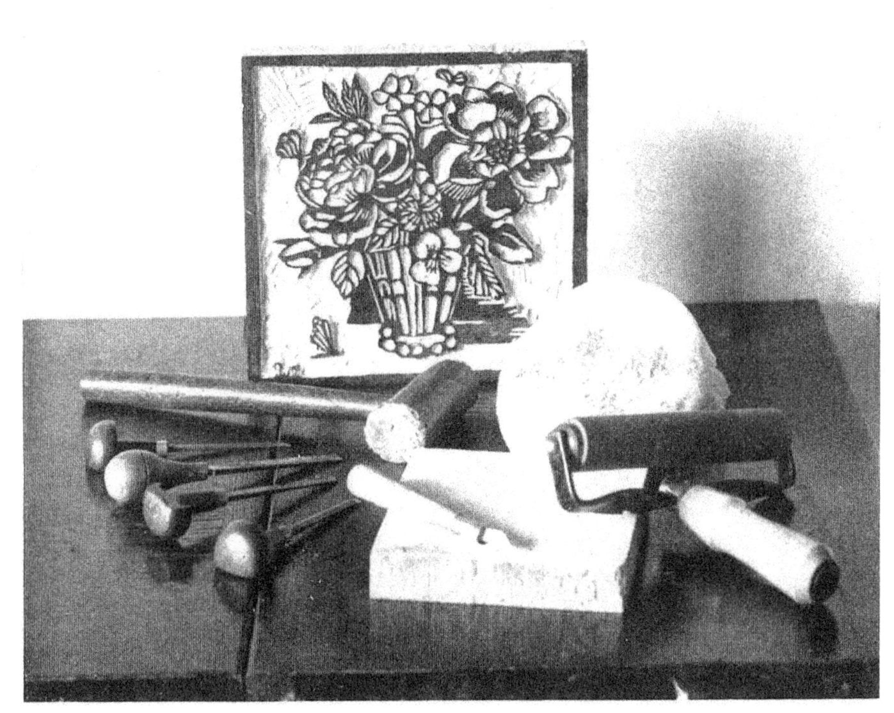

Materials used in Woodcutting, showing Woodblock inked ready for printing.

There and Back in Three Months

From Sydney to The East - With A Note On Expenses

The Home, Vol. 7. No. 10. October 1926

The heat of Sydney drove us to the tropics. We two left about December 20th with a destination unknown, even to ourselves. All we had provided was a ticket each to Singapore, a cabin trunk, two suitcases, a rug or two, and the right to break our journey where we wished.

We called at Brisbane and then Gladstone for horses, both distinctive Queensland towns, with the usual meat works much in evidence. Ten days after leaving Gladstone we arrived at Macassar, in the Sulawasi. Here we decided to leave the boat for a couple of days and then go on to Bali, an island near Java. Macassar introduced us to the cloth-less bed, bath-less bathroom, infantile lavatory and the Dutch wife, all four spotlessly clean. Our hotel expenses for two, inclusive, were twenty guilders a day, and a guilder is one and eightpence.

There is not much to see in Macassar - the usual native and residential quarter and, some miles away, a waterfall and scenery which is cool. We made arrangements here for our Bali trip. This took the boat twenty-four hours. The one drawback about visiting Bali is the landing. Buleleng, the port, is an open roadstead and one must beware of the western monsoon, as then no landing is possible. It was late at night when we arrived, but found a fishing boat, seemingly full of natives, waiting for us. They soon packed us in with our two suitcases and ten minutes later we landed. A car with a native driver-guide was waiting and drove us through the native town to Singaradja, the residential quarter, where we put up at the Government rest house, there being no hotels in Bali. Here we stayed the night, the charges being from seven to ten guilders. All the rest houses were clean and good. The Government fixes the tariff.

In the morning we started on our tour, stopping often to see the ins and outs of temples, one of which had a sacred fish in a pond. It had long fins like legs, on which it seemed to walk as we fed it with banana. The women of Bali are beautiful, but the men of the island still carry the kris. At Denpasar, in the south, we had the dancing girls perform. They were two little persons about eleven years old, gowned to the feet in tightly swathed silk and flower crowned. They were accompanied by some dozen men with native musical instruments. The dancing is not nigger, but is posturing in heroic attitudes, telling the story of some great deed. The dancers are too old to amuse after they are fourteen years. It is a mother-to-daughter business.

In Bali, as in biblical days, the women go to the well to draw water, balancing the pots on their heads. The men spend their days cock-fighting. There is much of interest to see. Kintamani, with the volcano and lake of Batur, Kloeng-Koeng with its native market, Sangsit the wonderfully preserved Hindu temple by the sea, the unsurpassed irrigation system for rice growing, and here and there the huge stone idols.

From Bali to Surabaya takes twenty hours. Here we made arrangements for a fortnight's tour by car and guide. Java seems full of children, scenery and volcanoes, but it has some important attractions. The Bogor gardens, with its orchid plantation, and where we saw the swan flower. The same town has a museum, where one can see the Christ fish. This is a mud fish that buries itself tail up, its bony structure forming a perfect representation of the crucifixion. Then there is Borobudur, a reconstructed collection of Buddhist monuments; also there is the marvellous museum in Djakarta. In Java we heard repeatedly, 'Here come Australians always in striped Fuji'. This trip costs about one hundred pounds. From Indonesia we went to Singapore.

Singapore has three hotels, one famed for its name, one for its social aspirations, and the third for its plumbing. Here it was necessary to see the Thai Consul, as we intended to go to Bangkok. Leaving Singapore we passed the proposed site of the naval base, which is as far from Singapore as Port Hacking is from Sydney. Our vessel called at the native States of Padang, Trengannu and Kelantan, all in the Malay peninsula. It is important to go by steamer only in the western monsoonal season, as all ports are open roadsteads and difficult. We also touched at several ports in Thailand before reaching Bangkok, notably Koh Samui, an island in the Gulf of Thailand, where are grown the best coconuts in the world. Koh Samui has its principal street, jewellers, eating houses, shops, post office and women weaving in the streets and all absolutely native.

After eight days we landed at Bangkok. This place is fairyland. Here is a market full of the most lovely things, known as the four-mile square. The waterways with the floating markets and shops on the water, and the temples with pointed gilded roofs and gaily coloured ceramic-ware decorations. The figures that guard the temple are mostly Chinese. One temple has a reclining gilt Buddha one hundred and twenty feet long.

Thailand has an absolute monarchy and there does not seem to be any labour trouble. The hotels cost about twenty ticuls a day and a ticul is two shillings and threepence.

From Bangkok we took another boat steaming along the coast of Thailand to Ream, a newly opened port in French Cambodia, a trip of some two days. Here we were met by a car arranged for in Singapore and started on our trip to Angkor. From now until we reach Saigon French is absolutely necessary.

Our first stop after Ream was Phnom Penh, the capital of Cambodia. It has subdued royalty. The next day we started for Angkor, lunching at a French inn where hunters of tigers and elephants stay, as the jungle is only fifteen miles from the hotel. Angkor is superb, right in the jungle and unrestored except in details. The real thing - a magnificent town and temple now past.

On our return journey we went as far as Phnom Penh by car and then travelled down the Mekong River to Saigon, a delicious trip of two days. Saigon (Ho Chi Minh city, Vietnam) is bright and French. Paris frocks can be had here free of duty. But it is Cholon, the Chinese town some five miles distant, that has all the attractions.

Our next port was Hong Kong. This famous mountain island came up to expectations. From it we made excursions to China proper, taking a small ferry running every ten minutes from Hong Kong to the mainland. A drive around the new territory of some seventy miles gave us a taste of China. We were not allowed to go to Canton (Guangzhou).

Macao was a very exciting little trip of four hours from Hong Kong. The boat was armoured, the engine quarters were steel barred and the captain's section and bridge were steel encased, with a Sikh guard and loaded rifle to let in only the right people, and all because of pirates. We went to Macao to see the place where Camoes wrote the *Lusiads* (*Os Luciadis*). He was sent to Macao for some political offence, and we saw the grotto that overlooked the town where he sat and wrote and fretted his life away. The facade of the cathedral of St Paolo is remarkable, as it was left intact by an earthquake, all the rest of the building being razed to the ground. Macao is Portugese and a backwash of the East, full of gambling, opium and other things.

Manila was our next port. Manila is very American. We asked a guide to take us to the principal places of interest. He took us first to the cemetery and then to the gaol. He said there was nothing else.

After Manila came Davao, in Mindinao. This is the principal hemp port of the Phillipines.

Here we saw Moros from the hills. They were dressed in skin hats covered in beads. Head-hunters, and they looked it.

At last we reached Thursday Island, vivid and dull, and then almost the best part of the trip: the Albany Pass and the wonderful Whitsunday Passage. The boat steams between interminable islands and the mainland of Australia, passing Dunk Island, our own Beachcomber's home forever. Whitsunday Passage is said to be more beautiful than the inland sea of Japan.

Brisbane we called at fleetingly, and then back to Sydney on March 20th. A three months' trip, travelling in ten steamers, money well spent and health never better.

Australia Ahoy!

Australia National Journal, January 1941

The beginning was a boat. It could have been the Ark, both species being represented. Unlike the Ark, it called at Ports. It first stopped at Brisbane to give the passengers a rest from each other. The 'Art' Library in that city is worth going to see.

After these few hours rest, it was the Boat and Blackouts again. The Ark had two classes on board - 'Us,' the Darwin crowd, and 'Those,' the going east 'Lot.' One of 'Us' was a bride; she was quite young and trusting. She was going to meet her 'Hubby' in Darwin. She was so worried, as she explained, 'I only saw him three times before I married him, and I don't know if I will know him again.' Her one clue was that he had red hair!

The East flying boat passed us in a great hurry; it wanted to get to Townsville before we did. It did. Townsville was still there when we got there; so were the crotons in the main street. The Flyer wagged her tail good-bye as we started off through the Barrier Reef for Thursday Island. This Reef business is a good idea, as it rarely leaves any chance for seasickness. Australia is proud of it.

Near Thursday Island the Ark 'lay by'; this means, no matter how much you grumble, you can't go ashore. So we were very pleased to reach Darwin, where all of 'Us' got off. Good-bye, Ark, Christianity was not born on a divided Boat.

Talking of Darwin, it was a great surprise. After reading some 'open season' literature on the place, we thought it would be frowsy and distinctly 'Fawn,' but, to the astonishment of us all, we saw on our arrival the most devastating swell people on the wharf. One was such a dazzle of laundry that we all gaped. It was said that he was a super colonel-general who had come to meet his wife. There were others as well, all in tropic suits. The ship on the other side of the wharf was haughty in grey. One expected to see an old black Tramp, with lots of angry, saucy seamen leaning against her sides, all in the attitude of 'striking.' But it wasn't like that at all.

Then a man came along and offered to see the luggage to the hotel; it was quite safe, as he was the undertaker. A healthy walk for a long time on the wharf, to reach the taxi stand. What a pleasure to hang out of the window to see the sights; a little disturbing at first, as Darwin's back door comes first; you work up to the front rooms. The streets were wide and building was racing along. The taximan pointed out a bank being built on a three thousand pounds piece of land. There didn't appear to be any dopey whites being led about by lubras, and it seemed to be a 'closed season' for piccaninies. The half-caste question wasn't too obvious either. Perhaps it had moved over to Melville Island. Anyway that is not a big island.

The hotel is a very spacious building, and has an office in it. All the Airways' travellers come to this hotel, so it is very smart, with evening clothes, cocktails and dances, all modern conveniences laid on.

There are some fine homes in Darwin, built for the climate. Hot in the 'Dry' and damp hot in the 'Wet.' There are also some 'First' families. There is much-liked Mrs Edwards and Mrs Bleeser. For culture, Mrs Litchfield, who is an aboriginal expert, puts Darwin on the map.

The aborigines mooching around Darwin looked cheeky and their trousers were dirty and seemed out of place. They were much nicer at Oenpelli (Arnhem Land); there the aboriginal had nice long legs and no trousers to speak about. The Oenpelli place is difficult to get to. You either fly or lugger. If you fly it takes about two and a half hours. If you lugg it is a matter of five days, should you be lucky.

The idea of the trip to Oenpelli was to see some aboriginal rock paintings. This little station is the starting place to see them. There are many rivers to cross before getting there, and no less than three Alligators (rivers of course) and herds and herds of water buffaloes wandering about. It's a rough, wild country. What were the rock paintings like? Well, they were excellent, mostly of every kind of fish, with turtles and other art-like creatures. Before leaving Darwin, with its good library, magnificent barracks and mighty ant hills, one item of social interest should not be overlooked - the men must number 100 to one woman.

The Ark had gone East and a jolly little State-owned cattle boat took its place. The Australian stewards were the highlights on this boat; they were excellent. It was rather a quiet trip to Wyndham, being that time of the year. This is the place where the cattle freezer is. The heat at Wyndham is of the burn and boil variety. The works do not operate in the summer; all the staff go to Perth. The cattle have all the luck to get frozen.

Next comes Derby, where the unfrozen cattle come on board. They are run in on runs, with electric prods to hurry them on. Derby had Baobab trees that grow nuts for the aborigines to carve and sell. It also has natives that have corroborees all night; really jolly ones like making noises imitating dingoes. Back to Nature is all right, but not at midnight, so the locals have to get up and throw stones at them to get any sleep. At Broome it was a 'lay-by,' so we didn't see the cemetery. This part of the coast of Australia suffers from tides; they run up and down about 30 feet, so it's 'lay-by' if the tide is down. It also has 'Willies,' technically known as typhoons; beastly things that are quite up to date in their inhumanity. If only de Rougement had kept to 'Willies' instead of turtles, he could have spread himself as he liked. Every one would have believed him. Anyway, his Turtle Island is near Derby, and is likely to be so, as it is big enough to defy a mere Willy.

After a few more 'calls in' and 'lay-bys,' Geraldton showed up. It's quite a smart place. Between it and Perth lies some of Western Australia's finest native flower country. Hence the Geraldton wax flower.

Arriving at Perth, to see its lovely 'Old London' Arcade and hear its musical aspirations.

Now comes a thrill. The Nullarbor train leaves Perth for Adelaide, so it's off through this dreadful desert, with its underground rivers, heat, sand and salt lakes. But first stop at Kalgoorlie - it's on the way. This town is exactly as you'd expect; every back yard looks as if the tenants hadn't waited to unpack when they moved in, but started to scratch for gold. No possibility left unturned. Back we go through the Nullarbor to glorious Adelaide. Let's leave it at that, and go around the coast to Melbourne. It's hateful to have to admit, but that Melbourne town has simply grown ahead; it is a magnificent dignified city. Anyone could feel proud of it, even if it isn't one's own country town. The drive to the aerodrome was through beautiful wide clean streets and fields.

A three-hour trip and the 'drome of Mascot turned up. Then came a drive to Sydney city through old boots, old slums, old smells and old rubbish. It would give any civic-minded person pleasure to bite a Sydney civic father. Oh for such good luck!

It's been just seven weeks since we met. Good-bye.

Colour

Art in Australia, 3rd Series, No. 9. October 1924

Like music, colour should not be haphazard but raised to the dignity of an applied science. It should be a science quite apart from and owing nothing to music. In every art the value of having all material well organised is obvious. Scientists have not given the artist the assistance which they might, and an understanding even of the most elementary principles by which colours are to be related is seldom found.

A 'set' palette has been made to serve this need by many of the great painters. Delacroix, France's greatest colourist, in his journal and in Megrafe's *Life of Eugene Delacroix* shows that he laid down for himself certain laws for colour. Comino Cennini in his little book on art gives a description of the work necessary for colours in gradation, the putting into jars of the colours mixed in their tones to correspond with each other and directions for the lights in which they are to be used.

It would be easy to enumerate name after name of artists who show by their works that they have used a 'set' palette, but it will suffice if Gauguin and Cezanne, both essential colourists, are referred to. In the Souvenirs of Paul Cezanne, Emile Bernard says: 'I understood at once that his work was guided by a law of harmony and that all these modulations had a direction determined in his mind in advance, in fact he must have proceeded as the old tapestry workers must have done, making the related colours follow one another until they met their contrast in opposition, but I felt that such a proceeding adopted with regard to nature would create as it were a contradiction, for every rational formula applies more freely and more easily to a work of art than to nature herself. It would be necessary in order to follow nature with the naivete of a child to have no prejudices, to act without deliberation and to observe and record equally free from personal bias. This was by no means Cezanne's method. Generalising from experiments (colour combinations) he applied these generalisations by a sort of convention so that he only interpreted and did not copy what he saw. His optics then were far more in his brain that in his eye.' Gauguin thrashed out the matter of colour by a long study of the old Japanese Masters; this is evidenced in his work, which is that of a magnificent colourist. The discoveries of all these artists have been the result of lifelong practice, aided by a special gift of seeing colour, but their researches as simple practical rules have not been tabulated and have been lost with death.

The necessity for the observance of rules of colour harmony exists in order to make it more likely that a given arrangement of colours will avoid the discordant and irregulated effects in our exhibitions, commercialism, etc., etc. Almost any music is pleasant to the ear in contrast to the average painting of today. Sir Joshua Reynolds says 'Every opportunity should be taken to discountenance that false and vulgar opinion that rules are the fetters of genius, they are the fetters only of men of no genius.'

So far, however, there is no guide as to which colours will harmonise. Black and white, which appeal to the intellect, and the use of quiet colours are an easy way to be in good taste. Colour, being emotional, can so easily be an abyss, but the use of subdued colours is not necessarily a mark of culture. It has been noted by keen observers that the lower the race in culture the less colour is used. The Australian Aboriginal is a case in point. Ask any very primitive peasant the colour of a tree and the answer is invariably white or black. From my own experience I have never found among the primitive races any original decorations with stronger colour than a dab of red raddle. The glow of colour suggested by the lava-lavas of the natives has come from Manchester. The finest colour I have found has been in Chinese and Persian articles.

The colour combinations that I now offer do not pretend to create, but are only skeletons to help build more intelligent and less chaotic results. These few ideas that I am giving do not aspire to any scientific value but are colour conjunctions which I have found are being used by most of the 'moderns'. I have based them on the solar spectrum to be found in Newton's 'Optiks'.

The analysis of the spectrum has been established only two centuries. Newton in the early part of his book ('Optiks') refers to only five colours, later on indigo and orange are added. In the following experiments I have omitted indigo. In red, yellow and blue we have the three primary colours which art represents in their emotional value; yellow which is peculiar to light, blue which is peculiar to shadow, produce opposite emotions but only give calmness of feeling by the absence of red, as red is a warlike colour and the sense of colour is not given in equal proportions of any two colours but by the management of one colour with another to produce a whole by their combination. This is Balance, and Balance is the adjusting of one colour to another until what is similar to both is asserted.

Tone too is the resultant translation of the intensity of colour; a certain amount of light is required to show any colour, and the quality of light will vary each colour. Also, with these colour combinations rhythm must be considered, as for instance dark red, pink, light blue, black, light green, cream and dark brown give a feeling of rhythm (W. S. George) and so on in many variations. Then there is simultaneous contrast and combination tones to consider, so that these hexachromic groups of colours appear very simple but require much study for their working.

In these groups I do not use black and white as actual colours but as 'additions'. In the matter of balance a combination of black may be made to balance a combination of the six colours provided the relative amount of the black is in true relative intensity to the colour. In black and white work to tone too high alters its colour relations and with work of these two colours tone is the principal thing.

In these colour groups I have made the three basic colours larger in mass than the intermediate colours, to insist on their importance as being the base for a colour scheme. Through the three primary colours we come to the binary combinations and then the complementary and synthetic combinations.

I start the first group with the spectrum according to Newton; it is as follows: You must know that pigments mixed together give different results to those that are so to speak mixed with light, this is the reason of the difference in the intermediate colours and from Newton's Triangle.

1st Hexachromic group	
(1) Ruby Red	(basic colour for artists)
intermediate	
(2) Primrose Yellow	intermediate
Yellow Green	
(3) Blue	intermediate
Violet	
Balance Pink (tone higher from Ruby Red)	

In all these groups 1 have added a seventh colour which is a tone higher than the basic note for balance and is really the beginning of another group.

FLANNEL FLOWERS

The picture was first designed on Balance. My group of colour is:

(1) Blue Green (Base)	
Blue ultramarine	intermediate
(2) Violet	
Vermilion	intermediate (tone higher)
(3) Maize Yellow	intermediate (tone higher)
Primrose Yellow	intermediate (tone higher)
Balance - pale blue-green	

Firstly I took the blue-green basic note for the leaves, then the balancing note, the pale flannel flowers, and lowered in half-a-note for their centres. I have omitted the other two basic colours and used black and white with the blue (intermediate colours). Background etc. I got from the use of the colours mentioned.

As can be seen by the above group, 'bright colours' are not considered.

Woodblocking as a Craft

Art in Australia, 3rd Series, No. 34. October-November 1930

Woodblocking is one of the easiest of all the crafts in the way of materials. Anyone can have them. A piece of wood, a knife, some ink, and a sheet of paper. That is the beginning - afterwards, as experience and ambition grows, better tools are demanded. It is a comfortable kind of craft. The material can be carried on in a small space. No huge piano, no etching press or potter's kiln. It is a friendly little craft, and, also, if you are lucky, a paying one. As this last remark will bring an appreciative audience, the following instructions may be interesting.

The wood will be the first consideration. The best kind for the work is that cut across the heart, which minimises the difficulties of grain. The knife can, at first, be a pocket knife, and a small gouge is also needed; a tube of black oil colour and laundry paper - or any that is slightly absorbent will do. To print the block - a tin tray to put the ink on and a photographer's squeegee to rub over the paper when it is on the block, and the amateur craftsman is set up.

As the wood-cutter gains more experience he will require better tools. Here is a list:

THE WOOD

Turkish box, sycamore or cherry, Tasmanian beech or Huon pine.

TOOLS

A three-cornered knife, made by the Japanese, gouges of different sizes, and a small wooden hammer.

INK

Lithographic ink. Prepare Indian ink or black oil colour.

FOR COLOUR PRINTS

Oil colours or prepare dry water colours with rice water.

PRINTING

Two squeegees, a stiff piece of cardboard covered with coarse muslin (called a baren), and a flat tray.

There are so many books written on how to do woodcuts that only the simplest directions will be given here.

First, the student determines if the prints are to be hand-coloured, coloured prints by pressing, or black and white only, if the colour is to be painted by hand or a black and white print desired, a key block only is cut, and no registration marks are needed. After the design has been drawn on the wood and the masses not to be cut out darkened, the outlines of all the edges are lined round with the knife, which is held sloping away from the edge so as not to risk breaking it. The gouge then digs out all the spaces not blackened, and here the hammer is useful to spare energy in pushing the gouge by chopping out the large spaces. This done, and the paper slightly damped and cut to the right size, the ink is placed on the tray, rolled with a squeegee until smooth, and then rubbed over the raised surface of the woodblock. The paper is then put on the inked wood and rubbed over with a clean squeegee until sufficient ink has been absorbed by the paper, which is then quickly pulled off the block, and the result will be shown on the reverse side. This is a key block, or black and white print.

If the print is to be hand-coloured it will be necessary to let it dry. The colour can be painted in any desired medium, and that is how Moronobu, the great Japanese wood colour blocker, worked.

For a colour print that is to be done by pressing, it is necessary to use a key block with registration marks. One way to do this, and the way the Japanese did it, is to put a cross at the top and at the bottom of the key block. These were printed with the design. Prints are printed off inclusive of the registration crosses to the number of colours required, and are then pasted onto blocks, printed side to the wood. Each block is then cut so as to ignore all but the shapes that are to carry the colour, not forgetting the registration marks. A colour is then rubbed over a block, the key-block print placed carefully on the registration marks, matching them exactly, and the block with print is then rubbed over with the baren or a squeegee. The other colour blocks are all cut in the same way and then printed with the registration marks until the key block is a finished colour print.

As can be judged by this method of hand-coloured printing, the design must be of the greatest importance—the simpler the better. The kind of wood used must be studied with the design. Soft woods will not carry very fine lines but depend on masses. Very fine lines look better in wood engraving. Woodblocking is quite a different craft; even the tools differ.

In the matter of printing, a press is often used, but the mechanical perfection that is gained is counter-balanced by the loss of artistic feeling that the hand-done work retains. Australia is flooded with press-printed wood blocks. They are, from the craftsman's point of view, almost valueless, having the same position that a hand-woven piece of tapestry has to a factory-made one. A craft is absolutely a matter of the combination of the hand and brain, and as soon as these partners are separated the result is incompleteness. Wood whittling is the most primitive of all crafts and loses most of its value when it accepts the aid of machinery to turn it into a commercial proposition.

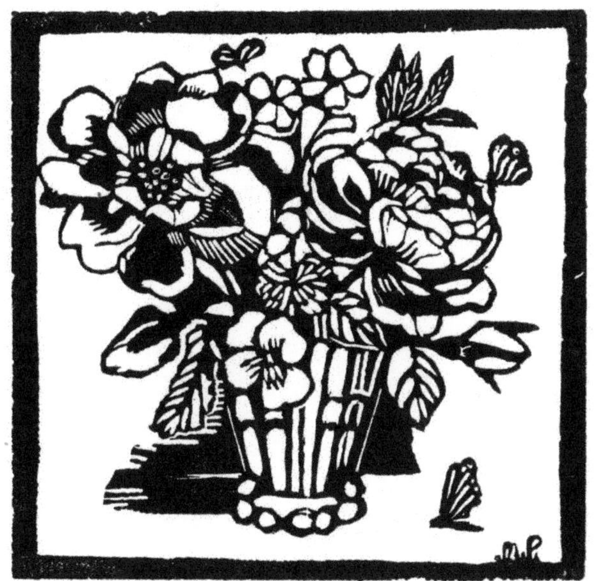

'Flannel Flowers', woodblock print, c1929, 24 x 26.4 cm, from Woodblocking as a Craft, *Art in Australia,* 1930.

Pottery as a Profession

Art in Australia, 3rd series, No.32 June-July 1930

In as short a manner as possible the making of earthenware will he described in this article. It cannot by reason of space be more than a resume of the craft. The kinds of clay, the making of the glaze, the colours for decoration, kilns, etc., all can be found in any good textbook. Only in the wheel throwing is it advisable to have a teacher, there are so many rules for manipulating the hands and fingers; but even in this there is always the original mind that gets over such difficulties. As a profession for women it is a wonder more do not take it up.

Working with a gas or electric kiln is expensive, therefore live out where wood is easily obtained. Much the best results are secured by using a wood kiln. The kind of wood burnt affects the glaze. Building a kiln is no bother, this article being written from actual experience. Digging up the clay is no worry, so that the two things that are absolutely necessary to make pottery pay are: the wood must be handy, and the clay to be had for the digging. As to the strenuous part of the work, if anyone knows any successful work that is easy, don't waste time reading this.

There are three great events in the life of a potter: one, the preparing of the clay; two, the making of the pot; and three, the final burning.

The first is a matter of digging the clay out of the ground, but surface clay does excellently for the craftsman. Chunks are dug up and put into a sack or any receptacle and taken to the pottery. There the clay, with its accompanying refuse of sticks, stones, etc., is thrown into a large wooden tub and half covered with water. This is all stirred together until it is of a very thick creamy consistency. Then three sieves of varying mesh are used. The coarsest is taken first and placed over a basin. Into this sieve is poured a moderate amount of the liquid clay. A short, stiff-bristled brush is now scrubbed vigorously over the mixture until only the big refuse is left. This is repeated until the basin is full. The same method is used with the two finer sieves until the clay is absolutely clean of all foreign substances. A piece of clean, rather open bagging is then used, the cleansed clay being poured into it. A bag is made by tying the sides into a knot at the top. It is then hung on a nail in a warm spot to drip and evaporate the water used in cleansing the clay. When the clay is dry, but not bone-hard, it is taken out of the bag and cut into large blocks with wire that has a piece of wood attached to each end. The clay is then banged on a board, piece on piece, thrashed and banged until every sign of an air bubble has disappeared. The texture of the clay with this treatment has become like ordinary block cheese - elastic and smooth. The clay is now a large mass, well wedged together, and is ready for the second event of the potter's life, the making of the pot.

Pottery can be made in different ways, the most primitive being that of doing it solely by hand, starting by rolling the clay into sausages, which are then placed one on top or alongside of each other, and pressing the joins together very firmly to get rid of any air holes, because an air bubble means a faulty pot. When the desired form has been comparatively reached a sharp piece of zinc or a shell is used to scrape away the surplus clay, because naturally the clay will be thick and clumsy working in this method, and the thicker the pot the longer and greater risk in firing.

Another method is that of taking the prepared clay, rounding it into a ball and throwing it on a quickly revolving wheel. This is the method that allows the craftsman the opportunity for absolutely beautiful and original work.

A third method is that generally used by factories. Putting the cleansed clay into water until it is the consistency of thick cream, it is then poured into plaster of paris moulds and allowed to stand a certain time to set and dry. The moulds, being in sections, are removed from the pots, leaving them of uniform thickness. This method allows of perfect duplication by the million, making the difference between the craft pot and the factory pot. China is made in moulds, as kaolin, from which it is formed, cannot be thrown on the wheel or used by hand. The pot by any method when dry is called green hard. In this condition it is now ready for the firing.

The next process will depend upon the type of ware that is wanted. If stoneware, there is no need for glaze, or second firing. The pots will be placed in the kiln, brought to about 2000° centigrade, then through an opening expressly arranged for, salt is thrown in, dissipates in the intense heat, and glazes the pots.

Magnificent examples of stoneware were made some years ago by the three brothers Martin. They regarded their work from a religious aspect, always having prayers before placing their pots in the kiln and before opening the kiln after firing. Alas, as each brother did one portion of the making of the pot, and fanatically guarded himself against anyone, even his brothers, seeing him work, when one of them died their pottery stopped. Their faultless creations can be seen in the Victoria and Albert Museum, London.

The pottery most frequently made by the craftsman is underglaze, which needs two firings. The green, hard pots are put into the kiln for their first firing without any extra cover, near each other, but not

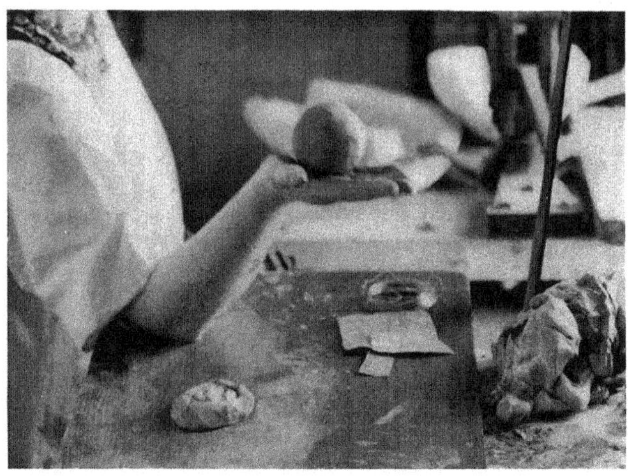

1. The ball of clay ready for throwing on to the revolving wheel.

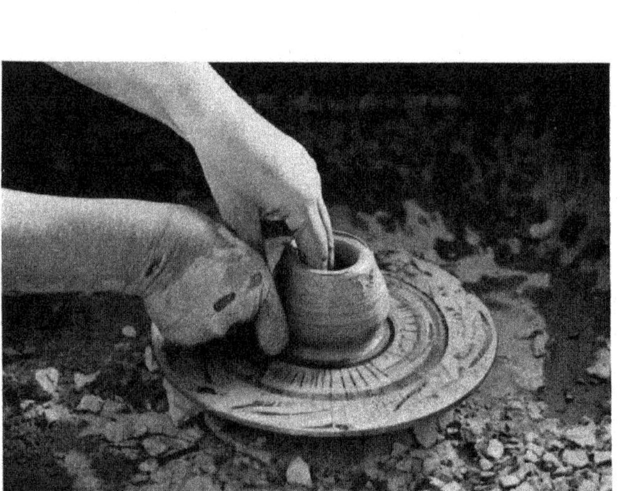

2. The opening of the pot—note the depression at the base of the pot. This is to allow the knuckle of the first finger to draw up the clay—the hands have drying clay on them. The wheel is stationary for the photograph to be taken.

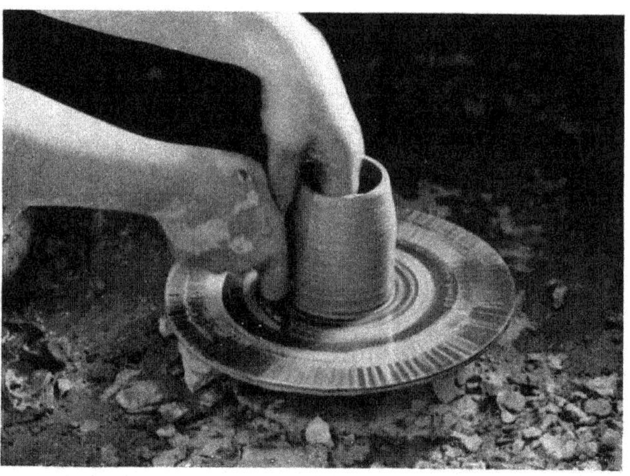

3. The pot is now straight, the clay having been drawn from the base. Note the position of the hands.

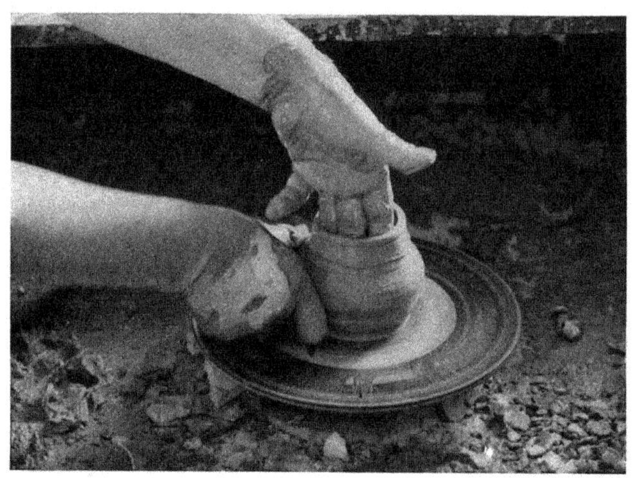

4. The forming of the swelling of the pot.

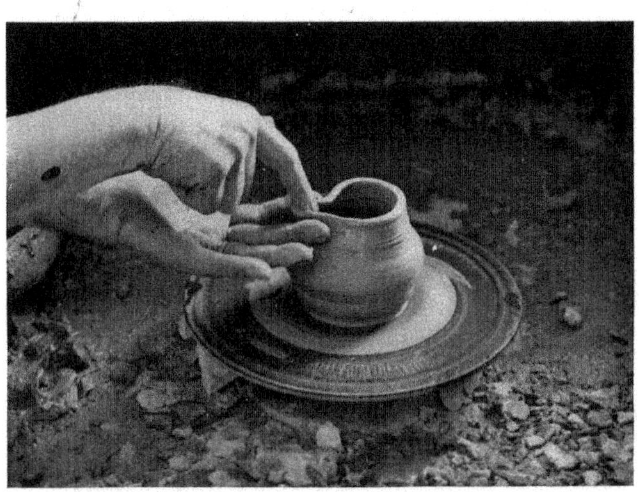

5. The making of the lip, with the wheel stationary as this is done without any movement.

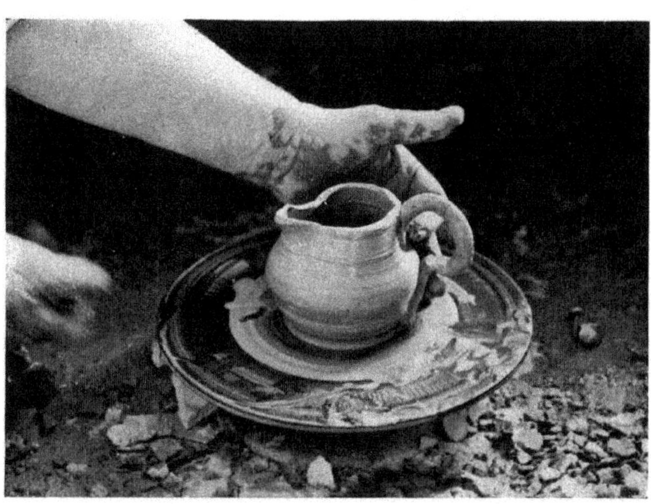

7. The handle is then pressed on by the fingers only, on to the crock, the form is made by the fingers.

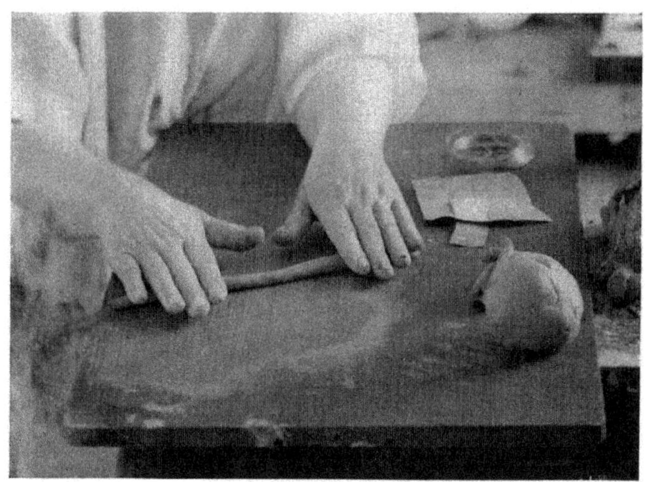

6. The making of the sausage for the handle. These sausages are also for all articles made by hand only.

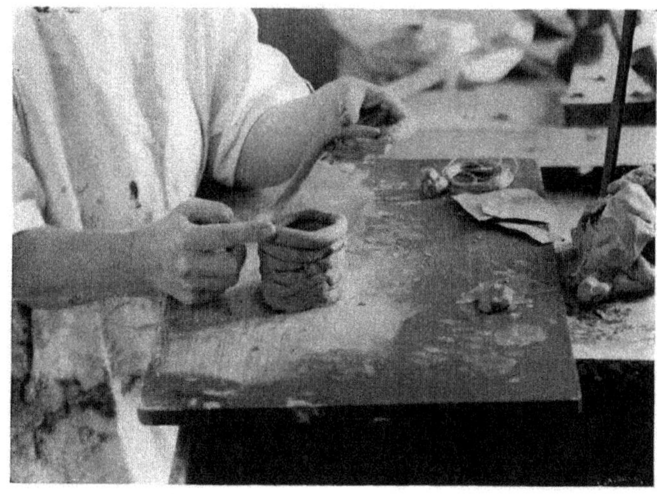

8. Making pots by sausages without a wheel. On the right hand side are pieces of zinc cut to any desired shape to shave down the thickness of the pot.

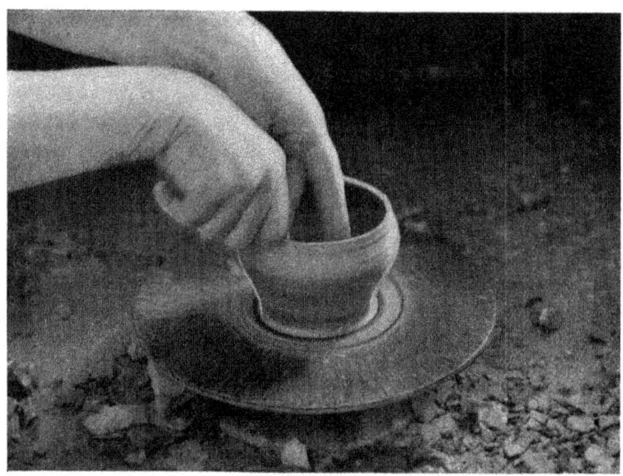

9. A pot being gently pressed into the shape of a wide bowl, the bent hand keeps the pot "true" while the upright presses the clay outward.

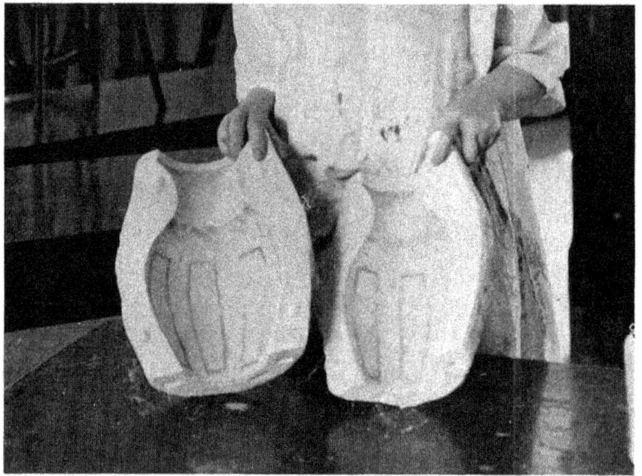

10. A section of a mould. The wet clay is poured into this, the mould is then well soaped, allowed to stay a little while then poured out. The remaining adhering clay remains a short while, the mould is then opened gently and the pot is ready for firing, etc. Note the keys on the mould. The fingers are pointing to them.

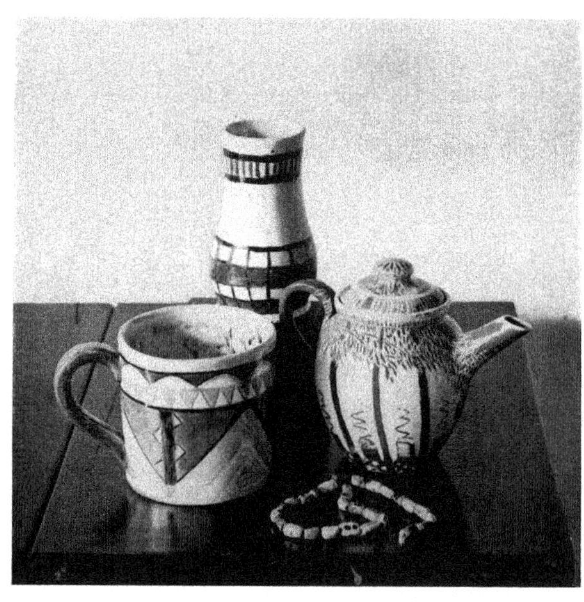

BRADFORD PHOTOGRAPH.

THREE pots. The mug is a mould, of Australian clay of Australian design, and made by an Australian, Mrs. Eyre. The other two were thrown on the wheel by Margaret Preston. The beads are made of clay with an under-glaze similar to those found in the tomb of Tutankhamen.

touching. The door is hermetically sealed, leaving a mark to show the peep-hole for testing the heat. The firing is very gradual for the green, hard pot, as any damp that may have been in the clay must be slowly dried out. Then when a certain heat has been reached - this depending upon the type of clay—the fire is drawn and the kiln, with pots inside, left to get quite cold. The pot is now ready for decorating. This done, it is glazed; that is, either dipped or has poured over it liquid of a milk thickness.

Now comes the final and third great event for the potter - the firing of the pot. The glazed pots are placed in covered cases called saggars, this to prevent the fire touching the glaze, which it would befoul. The opening of the kiln is again closed up, leaving the mark for the spy-hole, and the firing restarts, not so carefully as for the green hard pot, but to a much higher temperature to make the glaze flux.

At a certain heat the spy-hole is used either to judge by eye the colour of the heat or to insert special cones which sag at given temperatures. When the desired heat is reached the fire is again drawn and the kiln left to cool. When quite cold the pots are taken from the kiln-finished.

There are a few craft potters working even now in Australia, but the tendency is to lean too much towards the commercial type of work. It is perhaps useless to point out that no good can come of the awful approbation of repetition. Leave well alone. Australia has a right to its own individuality. Only original work should receive applause in such a young country. There's plenty of clay in Australia. Just get to it, someone, and originate.

Some Silk Screen Methods

Society of Artists Book 1946-47, Ure Smith 1947

Silk screen art belongs to the early Chinese centuries. It seems to have fallen out of favour for a long time, but is now having a renaissance. It is a craft that allows of both commercial and artistic achievement. There are at present about five or six different ways of working on the silk screen. Two or three will be discussed fully, the others only touched on. One dealing with the photographic method used mainly for fabric painting will not be considered; those that are explained can be used by any interested person. All the materials mentioned in them can be purchased in Australia.

MATERIALS

1. Organdie, or flourmillers' silk of various meshes.
2. Printers' ink (lithographic ink, in most colours, or oil colours, or Fox Bros. screen paint.)
3. Squeegees, sharp knife (stencil preferably).
4. Rollers (printers' proof rollers), made of gelatine.
5. Acetone, stopping-out lacquer (Taubman's brushing lacquer, black).
6. Cornflour, or china clay and lithotone.
7. Davis tube glue (other brands will do).
8. Three-pronged drawing pins, turps., meth. spirits, petrol, shellac, boiled linseed oil.
9. A paint scraper or very wide palette knife.
10. Profilm paper glasseine, architects tracing paper (prepared), or any strong paper that stands oil or varnish to make it transparent.
11. Frames, board for fixing frame on.

TO MAKE A SQUEEGEE

Take three pieces of flat wood, two to be 2 inches high and 1/2 inch thick, one to be 1 and 1/4 inches high and 1/4 inch thick; a piece of rubber, 2 inches high, 1/4 inch thick; length of squeegee, 4 inches, 6 inches, or any size needed.

TO MAKE THE SCREEN

First, a frame of wood, similar to those used for stretching artists' canvas, but no keys or bevel needed. Pin well with drawing pins the material over the side and back of the frame. Mix shellac with methylated spirits (allow to stand for some hours to dissolve) to make a sticky liquid. Brush over the material on the edges of the frame, allow to dry. Remove drawing pins.

BASEBOARD

1 inch 5 ply board, 1 inch wider than the screen. A piece of wood at one end to screw to frame to be about 1 inch wide, 3/4 inch high.

Screw the silk or organdie screen on to the hinge attached to wood; this gives a slight incline to the silk screen. A leg attached to the baseboard raises the screen and enables paper, designs, etc,, to be put underneath the screen. The leg must be able to be laid flat when not wanted.

TO MAKE LITHO INK

To make litho ink a particular consistency for some methods, take about a dessertspoon of litho printing ink, 1/2 dessertspoon of china clay or cornflour. Mix with a few drops of boiled oil, add a little turps, if too thick. Should be consistency of boiled custard - runs off knife quickly. Or use Fox Bros. Screen paint (prepared). For stop-out lacquer, if it gets too thick, use lacquer thinner or acetone.

REGISTRATION MARKS

There are various ways to keep the design in register:

1. Make a box of the design on the screen and fit paper exactly.
2. Mark on original design a cross, let half be on the cardboard on baseboard and the other half on the design.
3. Always remember to put the registration marks on the silk screen drawing to be printed.

PAPER

Paper for stencil, glasseine, architects' tracing paper, with a wash of shellac mixed with methylated spirits. Profilm or any strong paper that can carry oil or lacquer to make it transparent. For printing paper a slightly absorbent and matt paper is most suitable. Never glossy.

Have newspapers and cardboard to put on baseboard, to make screen and printing paper meet

BOOKS FOR REFERENCE

1. 'Silk Screen Colour Printing' (Harry Sternberg)
2. 'Silk Screen Stencilling as a Fine Art' (Biegelsen and Cohn)
3. 'Silk Screen Methods of Reproduction' (Bert Zahn)

METHODS

PROFILM METHOD

This is a method of cutting stencils and adhering them to the screen and printing through these stencils. Have the key design with the colours well spaced out and registration marks placed on it. Draw design through on to screen. Lift up screen and with drawing pins fix film over key design, shiny side up.

Cut around shape of stencil to be printed with sharp knife; profilm has two thicknesses; cut lightly so as not to cut bottom layer. Take away drawing pins. Put down silk screen on top of profilm and design and lightly iron with warm iron. This is for shellac profilm. For white profilm damp with acetone.

Take away design, put paper to be printed on to the baseboard, put registration marks on screen design, put sticky paper around screen design (under screen).

Put prepared ink in blobs at end of design, take squeegee in both hands and draw through screen paint on to open spaces. Lift screen and remove printed paper. Put fresh paper down and print as many copies as wanted. Repeat entire process for each stencil. Organdi or silk for this process. Use screen paint (Fox Bros.), or prepared paint.

FREE HAND SILKSCREEN METHOD - NO STENCIL CUTTING

Registration Marks - Have key design with large masses of colour. Put design under screen on sheet of cardboard. Pencil on screen the shape of the pattern to be printed, and whole design. Take away design and put paper to be printed underneath. Put sticky paper around design. Stop out all unwanted spaces. Use printing ink (paint) without filling, or screen paint. Put paint on glass slab, roll the gelatine roller in it until paint is smooth on roller.

Roll over screen, take away printed paper; put down fresh and repeat process for further colours. Always clean screen for new colours. This process is better if used with a wide mesh of flourmillers' silk. If the mesh is very open, a wash of lithotone and water over the whole design fills spaces. Allow the lithotone to dry and brush off with a stiff brush parts to be printed. Cover over the lithotone areas to be stopped out with the brushing lacquer. Acetone cleans all.

STENCIL METHOD WITHOUT PROFILM

Have key design, colours to be well marked. Draw through on to screen. Put stencil paper over design (glasseine, etc.) Draw design on glasseine, remove key design. Cut out on glass the stencil to be printed; put under screen on to the cardboard. Put adhesive tape round design on screen (underneath). Stick stencil to the screen with thin lacquer (underneath). Put paper to be printed with registration marks on it on cardboard on the baseboard. Rub over the stencil with screen paint with squeegee. Remove printed paper; repeat full process for further prints. Silk and organdi for this process.

SILK SCREEN METHOD - NO STENCIL NEEDED

Put design under screen. Draw design in pencil on screen. Take away design, put sticky paper round design on screen (under screen). Draw round shapes to be printed with lacquer. Stop out these shapes with lacquer; put paper to be printed under screen, put on screen design screen paint at end of drawing. Draw across with paint squeegee, remove printed paper.

Repeat full process for further prints. Always leave screen clean from ink. Colour can be superimposed. Other ways can be used to get different effects.

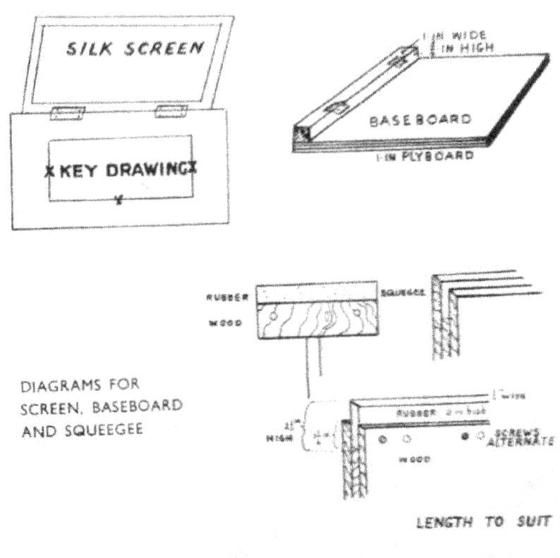

Preston's diagram for this article,
Society of Artists Book 1946-47,
Ure Smith 1947.

Artists' Groundwork

Society of Artists Book 1944, Ure Smith 1944

Every picture-making artist should have at least an elementary knowledge of his materials; of what they are made, and how to apply them. The war has left Australia without many of the commercial products that the artist has depended on. One is the prepared canvas - the lack of which has driven some artists to use various substitutes without any knowledge of the material or even how to prepare it. For this reason the following hints are given. As they are from personal experience, they may be useful:

1. The base
2. Paints
3. Mediums for painting
4. The facing.

1. BASES

(Canvas, Cardboard, Masonite, Wood). An artist's canvas is a cloth prepared for the use of picture-making. It is made of cotton, hemp, or flax. All materials must be free from dressing. Otherwise they must be soaked overnight in cold water and pegged out to dry.

Cotton

Sail cloth (duck). English cloth is preferable to Australian, as the latter often shows small black threads when damped. The facing covers these, but they are still there. I have work done years ago on duck; it holds well.

Flax - This makes a fine linen canvas. Osnaberg (kitchen towelling) has a very reliable surface, but some of the irregular threads with which it is woven show up as knots when dampened. These cover in the facing.

Hemp

Unbleached linen. Makes a coarse canvas and is useful for large canvases. Hemp is an Asiatic herb and has a tough fibre.

Twill Sheeting
Made from linen is excellent.

Cardboard
When one-eighth of an inch thick is good. It does not shrink or buckle, nor is it influenced by atmospheric onditions. It should be backed by another piece of cardboard of the same thickness. I have a picture painted some thirty years ago on this material; it has been subjected to very bad treatment, but has not moved in colour and is in perfect technical condition.

Masonite
Made from the leaf of the yellow pine. The wood fibres are torn apart by exploding the small pieces at high pressure. It is then compressed on to wire screens, which make the pattern on the rough side. There arc three thicknesses; the thickest is the best for artists' work. Masonite has been proved to be 'grub' proof and does not sweat. A picture painted on it that has been out of doors for three years in all weathers, shows no sign of discolouration.

Wood
Dangerous, unless certified seasoned for at least twenty-five years. Useful to fasten thin linen or muslin onto.

2. PAINTS

Keep the palette with as few colours as possible.

Table of Colours for Grinding		About
Flake and Cremnitz White	Use poppyseed oil	7-25%
Naples Yellow: Permanent	Use raw linseed oil	15%
Chrome Yellow: Darkens	Use raw linseed oil	20%
Cadmium: Permanent	Use raw linseed oil	40%
Raw Sienna: Darkens	Use raw linseed oil	100-200%
Burnt Sienna: Permanent	Use raw linseed oil	40-60%
Yellow Ochre: Permanent Slightly warm before grinding	Use raw linseed oil	30-80%

Indian, Venetian Red: Permanent	Use raw linseed oil	40%
Vermillion: Poor	Use raw linseed oil	7-25%
Cadmium Red: Poor	Use raw linseed oil	40%
Carmine: Bad		
Madders: Fleeting		
Ultramarine: Permanent	Use raw linseed oil	50-150%
Slightly warm before grinding		
Alazarins: Permanent	Use raw linseed oil	40%
Cobalt: Good	Use raw linseed oil	50%
Cerulean Blue: Good	Use raw linseed oil	50%
Prussian Blue: Permanent	Use raw linseed oil	100%
Oxide of Chromium: Permanent	Use raw linseed oil	100%
Raw Umber: Very good	Use raw linseed oil	80%
Ivory Black: Permanent	Use raw linseed oil	80-100%

Materials to Grind the Colours

As nearly all the powders are commercial, they have a body in them that does not need the aid of wax to thicken them.

A strong tin tray, plate glass or pestle and mortar.

A rolling-pin or strong squeegee.

A spatula or palette knife.

Always drop the oil in slowly. Mixture should be the thickness of tube colours. If needed to aid in drying, a minimum of sugar of lead can be added.

Facing

All artists' bases must be faced.

MATERIALS FOR THE FACING

Glue

Never boil glue. Should be a skin or animal glue. Fish glue cracks; vegetable glues peel. A good sheet glue should have no fractures, be clear. Should double its weight in water; does not break easily or go to pieces or discolour.

Sheet Gelatine

Transparent, dissolves in hot water. Holds well but must be used sparingly, as it may crack. Davis A Grade Gelatine (powder), an animal glue, is excellent.

Australian Russian Glue

Good. Imported not so good as it is often a bone glue.

Scotch Glue - Good. Cox No. 7, powdered glue, made from hides.

3. MEDIUMS FOR PAINTING

(Oil, Boiled and Raw Linseed Oil) - Raw linseed sun-thickened oil. Put the raw oil on plates in the sun, about 1/4 in. deep; stir from day to day. Takes about three weeks. Should be clear in colour and thickness of golden syrup. Turpentine-Wood. Made from various pine trees. Never use mineral turpentine, which is made from petroleum products.

Varnish

Dammar gum (soft) made from the dammar trees; mastic gum, made from the mastic trees. Take one part of either gum to four parts turpentine, hang the gum in a muslin bag to the depth of 1-inch in the turps. Keep tightly covered. Takes about two days to dissolve.

Venice Turpentine

From the larch tree. Not so good as it is darker. Is very reliable. Venice turps (one part), wood turps (five parts). Put together in a pot, in a bath of very hot water, until they melt together.

These varnishes are not for varnishing pictures.

Copal

A generic name for various resins; some hard, some soft, some acid. It is dangerous to use unless the resin used is mentioned.

A good painting medium is: One part wood turps, one part dammar or mastic varnish, one part sun-thickened raw linseed oil.

4. FACING

Never dry by artificial heat.

Materials

French chalk, zinc white or white lead, glue size, sun-thickened oil or boiled linseed oil, a mason's trowel (about 6in. long by 3in.), house-painter's brush (about 2in. across).

Method

Put the materials together as in order placed. Have glue size one to twelve parts water (1lb glue, 1 quart water). Add French chalk, zinc white or white lead, each in equal parts. Add two parts of boiled linseed oil. Drip the oil in as for a salad. Mixture should be the consistency of a batter. Add more glue water if necessary.

Method for Facing

(1) Brush over the base a thin wash of glue water. Allow to dry for twenty-four hours. (2) Brush facing mixture across the gummed base with a wide brush. (3) Scrape off in one direction with the trowel. Leave a very thin covering. Allow to dry for one hour. (4) Same method only covering from the opposite direction, scrape off as before. Repeat twice.

If too absorbent when dry cover lightly with equal parts cold congealed glue and boiled linseed oil. Do not use the faced base for a fortnight. The longer the better.

All materials can be bought locally.

Crafts that Aid

An in Australia, 3rd Series No 77. November 1939

This article is a personal one. It is partly reminiscent and partly it deals with the immediate future.

In 1916, British shell-shocked and injured soldiers started pouring into England. This necessitated hospitals that were fitted to deal with their maladies. Many cases, such as those with shock to the nerves and with injured limbs, had long intervals between the various times when they were seen by the doctors and by the administration. This circumstance demanded the services of persons who were able to interest the men, and to aid the doctors in ways that did not come under the heading of 'nursing.' Some of this work took the form of handicrafts.

My own experience was gained in a shell-shock hospital situated on Dartmoor, England. The building had been an agricultural college, and it was requisitioned by the Government for the use of soldiers suffering from nerve trouble. This was the main object of the hospital, but there were also cases of twisted hands and stiffened limbs that had to be treated. The hospital was for the rank and file, and not for officers.

The men would arrive in fortnightly batches from the war areas. My work was to take from twenty-five to thirty men every two or three weeks. These the various doctors would bring down to the shed known as the pottery. This outhouse was originally the dairy of the agricultural college. The work was under strict supervision of the doctors. It consisted of basket-making for twisted and stiffened hands; of pottery for the shell-shocked men. This was to aid them to regain confidence in their own abilities as well as to interest them while they were waiting for their cures. There were others who came to the shed with complaints that allowed them only to amuse themselves. These did monotypes, batik, and other handicrafts.

Perhaps the most valuable of them all was basket-weaving. This simple craft has the greatest right of all the handicrafts to the name, as it is about the only one that cannot be carried on by machinery. The great help that basket-making gives to twisted hands and stiff arms is acknowledged by doctors who have worked in war hospitals. Pulling of the canes and holding and separating the rods used muscles and fingers that had become stiff and hard. Another thing that helped was the simplicity of the craft. It did not worry tired brains, and took very little concentration to obtain a good result. These facts place basket-making well on the way to being one of the most useful of the handicrafts for war-time work.

For those who know nothing of this art, a few explanations and illustrations might be of interest. The materials are inexpensive and substitutes can be easily procured. When cane gave out at the hospital, young rose shoots, raffia, and Paddy's lucerne were used. In fact, any branches that were strong and supple enough to twist were made into baskets. When these baskets were sold to the local housewives of Newton Abbot (the nearest town), some of the women complained that the baskets 'started to shoot' on shopping expeditions, and were a little conspicuous; but it was pointed out to them that these were really 'war baskets,' so no money had to be given back.

As regards the materials for this work, only a few tools are necessary - a basket-maker's bodkin, a pair of sharp shears, a picking knife, and a basket-maker's iron for knocking the cane together. For a simple basket, two kinds of rods are employed. Some of these are young and pliable. The others are older branches, known as 'sticks.'

For larger baskets, stronger canes and a different method are used, but it can be seen how the hands are used in manipulating the sticks. The pulling and stretching of the fingers all help in the recovery of lost suppleness. It is suggested here that lessons could be taken from the blind, so that when a time comes there will be found persons who will be able to help when necessary.

At the hospital on Dartmoor, some of the men went on to advanced lessons in this craft. They are now earning their living making fish and clothes baskets, which take strong hands and careful work.

Next to basket-making, pottery work was of the greatest assistance. This craft helped cure in many ways. For one thing, it gave an easy and interesting occupation. For another, it restored confidence, when the patient found that he could make things that his doctor could not. Again, it gave healthy exercise and allowed the brain to work out original ideas and put them into practice. Perhaps the great thing was, that, at the end of the labour, the patient possessed an object that even the doctors wanted, and that he could raise money on if he so wished.

The method of making pottery by these shell-shocked men was simple in the extreme and had no connection with public money-making. As the hospital was out on the moors, there was no gas or electricity for firing. There was no factory at which to buy ready-prepared clay, and there were no shops to run to when the glaze supplies failed. It was a self-made affair from beginning to end.

The first thing that had to be seen to was the making of a kiln. It was found that amongst the patients were bricklayers, who were capable, under strict supervision, of laying the bricks. This was done from a simple plan of a small brick kiln, of the kind generally used as an experimental one for brick factories. It had been proved quite successful in Cornwall, where I had worked with my friend Gladys Reynell.

After the kiln was built, the next thing was to get the clay. This meant that all the patients who could walk would carry pieces of sacking or bags and shovels. As the hospital was in Devon, the finding of clay was no bother. (By the way, there is plenty of rough clay in our Australian ranges - not suitable for commercial pottery perhaps, but quite useful for amateur work). At the end of the walk, the men would hump clay back on their backs, and then go back to the shed. Sometimes when the men were not able to carry the clay, a cart and horse would be begged from the farmer nearby, but generally we humped it back ourselves. When the clay arrived at the shed it was thrown into an old wooden tub and covered with water. The next day it was stirred by hands that needed such gentle treatment as the pressing together of some such substance as liquid mud. Memory goes back to one poor 'Tommy' who had decided that his hands could not move. When they were gently 'pushed' into the mud, he quickly decided to pull them out and use them on the 'pusher,' who was myself. The doctor rushed to the rescue and took away a soldier who had been partly cured of a difficult complex.

After the men had mixed the mud and water to the consistency of very thick cream, they scrubbed it through three different sieves to be thrown away. The clean clay was then put into bags and hung in the sun to allow the water to drip out. After some days it was brought into the pottery shed and put on the table, where it was beaten and thrashed to get all the air out, and to set the clay in a fine smooth mass for work.

Then the wheel had to be made, and the wheel was as primitive as the rest of the materials. It consisted of an iron shaft with a circular flat piece of iron attached to the top. This shaft had another length of iron joined to it half-way. The iron had a handle at its free end, which turned the shaft around and so revolved the circular plate at the top. The whole was enclosed in a box, which had a shelf and ledges that held the clay ready for throwing. One soldier would turn the handle, while another threw on the wheel. It would hardly seem possible that turning a wheel would start a cure in a case of badly shaking nerves, but this happened. Many doctors visited the pottery shed either to see their patients, or to study how the scheme worked. There were also different visitors. Amongst these was John Galsworthy, who edited a kind of shell-shock paper. When Galsworthy's visit was expected, the most shaking patient was put to turn the wheel. This man had been for two years a martyr to the most convulsive shaking. It was discovered that he had one decided trait - an extreme personal vanity. When Galsworthy arrived with secretary and photographer complete, this patient was asked to try and keep still, and to look at a new pair of silk laces that had been put in his shoes. He did so, exercising tremendous will so that the photograph should not be a failure. His doctor counted the seconds that became minutes, and another patient was taken away, well on the road to a cure that later became permanent. This man's work is now in the War Museum in London.

Many men did not like throwing on the wheel. They were shown how to make objects by winding sausages of clay together. Some of these men produced fantastic animals and grim creatures that would have turned Dali green with envy. The doctors found these efforts interesting, and would try to get the men to part with them, but none of them would do so. They are to be found in unexpected places, such as miners' homes and policemen's barracks, where they remind their owners of the pottery shed at Seale-Hayne Hospital on the Devon moors.

The kiln was used once a week. The firing was of wood or coal, and the glaze used for the pottery was of borax. It did not take long to cook the pots. Twelve hours, or perhaps a little longer, were enough, as the clay was of a low-firing grade. The morning the bricked-up door of the kiln was opened saw a scene like a village fair. Doctors with their patients of the pottery shed, and others not associated with the shed, would turn up in full force to see the results. The bidding of the soldiers to try and get possession of the precious objects was amusing. The doctors would offer large sums to try and get some, but they could hardly ever, if at all, part the pots from their makers. The kiln was later pulled down. Alas, it seems as if it may have to be rebuilt for other 'Tommies.'

Other crafts interested the men. One was simple dyeing. This meant long walks on the moors, looking for plants that would give dyes. Sorrel was found to give a yellow, and the bulbs of the white iris a good black. These were brought back to the shed, cooked in jam tins, and later fixed with a mordant of common salt, alum, or some simple chemical. Thus the dye would not come out of the cloth when it was washed.

Dyeing was used in conjunction with batik work. A piece of unbleached calico would have a simple design drawn on it. This was retraced with hot wax, which was contained in tins that had lips to them. These were kept liquid over methylated spirit stoves. When the design had been waxed, the cloth was put into the boiling dye for a few minutes; then taken out and washed with soap and water. Any wax left on was scraped off with a knife. Cushion covers were generally the greatest extent of our ambitions. Woodcutting was another craft that helped things along. There being no money for anything, everything that could be made to do was used. Cigar-box lids, old pieces of furniture that could be cut into shapes; any wood that had a fine grain - all was gratefully accepted.

The paint would be rubbed on an old tray with a photographer's squeegee, and then over the upstanding design of the wood. A piece of dampened paper would be put on this, and rolled with a clean

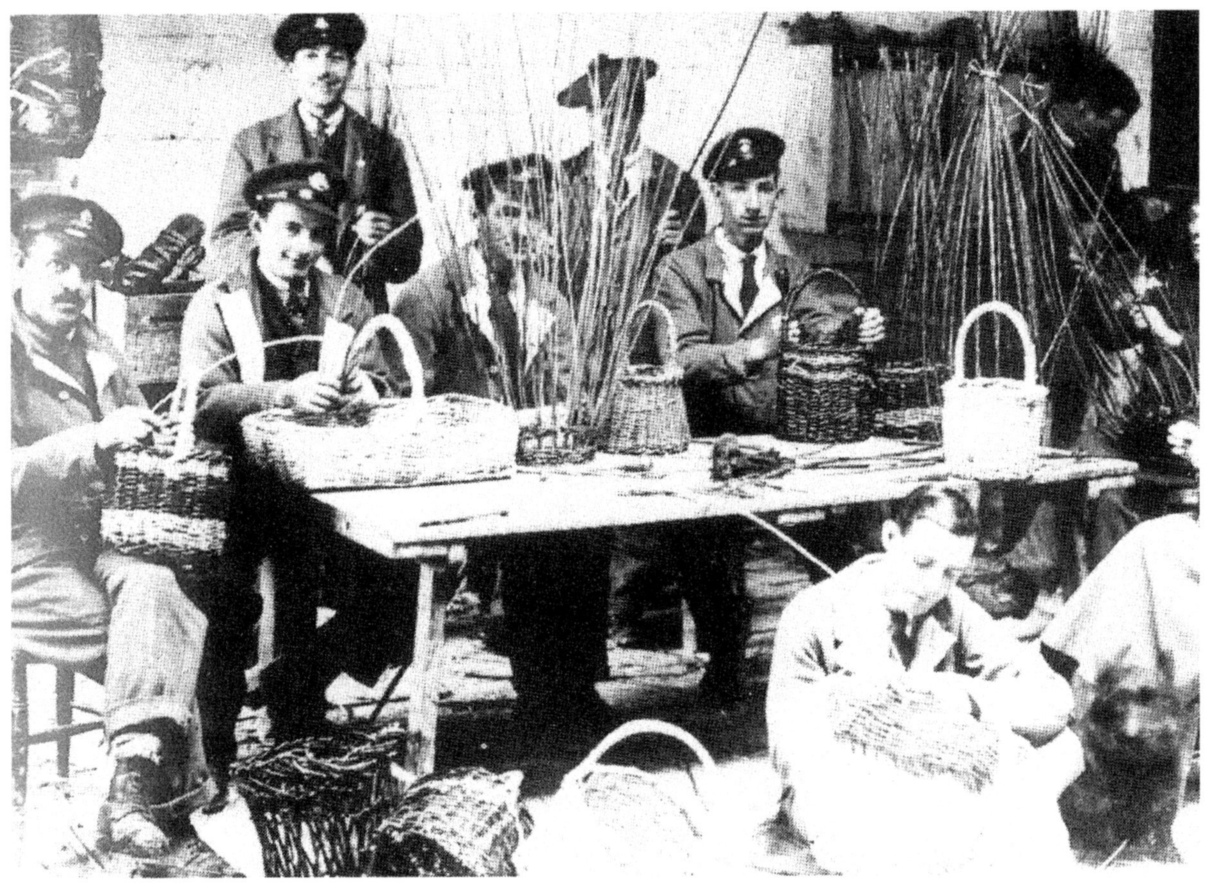

1918: Some of the shell-shocked soldiers to whom Margaret Preston taught basket-weaving at the Seale-Hayne Neurological Military Hospital, Devonshire (UK). Preston is out of camera (right) next to her terrier 'Little Jim'.

roller. The paper was taken off, and the results shown around for criticism. Monotypes were also popular, as they caused no excessive expenditure of energy. This craft was done with a small piece of plate glass, zinc or copper, a soft hairbrush, a roller, a rag, and some blotting paper. The worker began by rubbing a little oil and paint on the glass. This he tried to get fairly even. Then he drew his design on to this, wiping out the white parts to be, and the highlights with the rag. Then he quickly placed a piece of paper on this drawing, rolled it over with his roller, and pulled it off the face of the glass. Many made Christmas Cards this way. The cards were of course unique, as it is only possible to get one copy by this method. Then there were other crafts to interest the men. Stencilling was one. All the crafts are better then the horrible work known as crewel work. The most pathetic thing was to see a big wounded soldier, plugging away in crewels at the motto, 'God Bless our Happy Home,' which was often to be seen in the war hospitals.

This is an article on 'crafts that help.' It is the moment to prepare for such work. As this is a personal article, it is not out of place to give advice on such matters. The Arts and Crafts Society are the people to be consulted. In New South Wales, Miss Florence Sulman, the president of this society, is always willing to help. She is extremely competent to do so.

INDEX